International Association for the Evaluation of Educational Achievement

TIMSS International Study Center
Boston College
Chestnut Hill, MA, USA

© 1997 International Association for the Evaluation of Educational Achievement (IEA).

Performance Assessment in IEA's Third International Mathematics and Science Study / by Maryellen Harmon, Teresa A. Smith, Michael O. Martin, Dana L. Kelly, Albert E. Beaton, Ina V.S. Mullis, Eugenio J. Gonzalez, and Graham Orpwood

Publisher: Center for the Study of Testing, Evaluation, and Educational Policy, Boston College.

Library of Congress Catalog Card Number: 97-69827

ISBN 1-889938-07-6

For more information about TIMSS contact:

TIMSS International Study Center
Center for the Study of Testing, Evaluation, and Educational Policy
Campion Hall
School of Education
Boston College
Chestnut Hill, MA 02167
United States

For information on ordering this report, write the above address or call +1-617-552-4521.

This report also is available on the World Wide Web:
http://wwwcsteep.bc.edu/timss

Funding for the international coordination of TIMSS is provided by the U.S. National Center for Education Statistics, the U.S. National Science Foundation, the IEA, and the Canadian government. Each participating country provides funding for the national implementation of TIMSS.

Boston College is an equal opportunity, affirmative action employer.

Printed and bound in the United States.

Contents

Introduction

Performance Assessment

The Third International Mathematics and Science Study (TIMSS), conducted by the International Association for the Evaluation of Educational Achievement (IEA), is the largest international comparative study of student achievement to date.[1] The purpose of the study, like that of IEA studies generally, was to learn more about the nature and extent of student achievement and the context in which it occurs, in order to inform policy decisions about schooling and its organization in the participating countries. TIMSS tested students in mathematics and science at five grades and collected contextual data from students, their teachers, and the principals of their schools.

Although student achievement was measured in TIMSS primarily through written tests of mathematics and science, participating countries also had an opportunity to administer a performance assessment, which consisted of a set of practical tasks in mathematics and science.[2] The performance assessment was available for administration to a subsample of the fourth- and eighth-grade students that completed the written tests.[3] Table 1 presents the countries that participated in the TIMSS performance assessment. Table 2 shows, for each country, the name of the assessed grades, together with the number of years of formal schooling that students in that grade had been exposed to, and their average age at the time of the TIMSS assessment.

This report presents the initial findings from the TIMSS performance assessment. Some 1,500 schools and 15,000 students from 21 countries participated, making it the largest international performance assessment yet conducted. The study was an enormous undertaking that has yielded an unprecedented store of information on how students around the world perform on a selection of practical tasks in mathematics and science.

[1] See Appendix A for a description of TIMSS.

[2] The development of the TIMSS performance assessment was greatly facilitated by the work of the Performance Assessment Committee.

[3] More specifically, the written tests were to be given to the two adjacent grades with the largest proportion of 9-year-olds, the two adjacent grades with the largest proportion of 13-year-olds, and students in the final year of secondary schooling. The performance assessment was administered to subsamples of students at the upper grade tested for 9-year-olds and the upper grade tested for 13-year-olds. For most countries, these were the fourth and eighth grades.

Countries Included in the TIMSS International Performance Assessment Report[1] Table 1

Eighth Grade

- Australia
- Canada
- Colombia
- Cyprus
- Czech Republic
- England
- Hong Kong
- Iran, Islamic Republic
- Israel
- Netherlands
- New Zealand
- Norway
- Portugal
- Romania
- Scotland
- Singapore
- Slovenia
- Spain
- Sweden
- Switzerland
- United States

Fourth Grade

- Australia
- Canada
- Cyprus
- Hong Kong
- Iran, Islamic Republic
- Israel
- New Zealand
- Portugal
- Slovenia
- United States

SOURCE: IEA Third International Mathematics and Science Study (TIMSS), 1994-95.

[1] Please see Appendix A, Figure A.1, for countries participating in other components of the TIMSS testing. Because low school participation led to a small sample size, performance assessment results at the eighth grade for Hong Kong are presented in Appendix B. Results for Israel are presented in Appendix B because within-school sampling procedures were not documented at the fourth and eighth grades; in addition, Israel had a small sample size at the eighth grade.

Table 2 Information About the Grades Tested

Country	Eighth Grade			Fourth Grade		
	Country's Name for Grade	Years of Formal Schooling Including Grade Tested[1]	Average Age*	Country's Name for Grade	Years of Formal Schooling Including Grade Tested[1]	Average Age*
[2] Australia	8 or 9	8 or 9	14.3	4 or 5	4 or 5	10.2
Canada	8	8	14.1	4	4	10.0
Colombia	8	8	15.8	.	.	.
Cyprus	8	8	13.8	4	4	9.8
Czech Republic	8	8	14.4	.	.	.
England	Year 9	9	14.0	.	.	.
Hong Kong	Secondary 2	8	14.2 **	Primary 4	4	10.1
Iran, Islamic Rep.	8	8	14.6	4	4	10.4
Israel	8	8	14.1 **	4	4	10.0 **
[3] Netherlands	Secondary 2	8	14.3	.	.	.
[4] New Zealand	Form 3	8.5 - 9.5	14.0	Standard 3	4.5–5.5	10.0
Norway	7	7	13.9	.	.	.
Portugal	Grade 8	8	14.6	4	4	10.3
Romania	8	8	14.6	.	.	.
Scotland	Secondary 2	9	13.7	.	.	.
Singapore	Secondary 2	8	14.5	.	.	.
Slovenia	8	8	14.7	4	4	10.9
Spain	8 EGB	8	14.3	.	.	.
Sweden	7	7	13.9	.	.	.
Switzerland (German)	7	7	14.1	.	.	.
United States	8	8	14.2	4	4	10.1

SOURCE: IEA Third International Mathematics and Science Study (TIMSS), 1994-95. Information provided by TIMSS National Research Coordinators.

* Computed from TIMSS performance assessment sample.

** Due to performance assessment sampling issues, average age is computed based on the main assessment sample (see Appendix A).

[1] Years of schooling based on the number of years children in the grade level have been in formal schooling, beginning with primary education (International Standard Classification of Education Level 1). Does not include preprimary education.

[2] Australia: Each state/territory has its own policy regarding age of entry to primary school. In 4 of the 8 states/territories students were sampled from grades 4 and 8; in the other four states/territories students were sampled from grades 5 and 9.

[3] In the Netherlands kindergarten is integrated with primary education. Grade counting starts at age 4 (formerly kindergarten 1). Formal schooling in reading, writing, and arithmetic starts in grade 3, age 6.

[4] New Zealand: The majority of students begin primary school on or near their 5th birthday so the "years of formal schooling" vary.

A dot (.) indicates country did not participate in performance assessment at the fourth grade.

THE NATURE OF PERFORMANCE ASSESSMENT

Performance assessment refers to the use of integrated, practical tasks, involving instruments and equipment, as a means of assessing students' content and procedural knowledge, as well as their ability to use that knowledge in reasoning and problem solving. The assessment task may be as simple as the routine use of a piece of equipment or as complex as an investigation combining manipulative and procedural skills and requiring higher-order thinking and communication. Performance assessment aims to provide students with a testing environment which is more "true to life" and "authentic" than the traditional paper-and-pencil written test, and, by providing them with equipment and materials to manipulate in a realistic problem-solving situation, attempts to elicit performances or behaviors which will be a more valid indication of the students' understanding of concepts and potential performance in real life situations.

Proponents of performance assessment argue that the practical nature of the tasks utilized in this mode of assessment permits a richer and deeper understanding of some aspects of student knowledge and understanding than is possible with written tests alone. These aspects include skills like weighing and measuring, the use of experimental or mathematical procedures, designing and implementing approaches to solve problems or investigate phenomena, and synthesizing knowledge, application, and personal experience into an interpretation of data.[4]

Performance assessment has captured the attention of teachers and policymakers for a variety of reasons. It reflects the current trend in many countries towards active, inquiry-oriented, hands-on teaching and learning. It is seen as a means of assessment that is educationally valid, psychologically and developmentally appropriate, and congruent with "constructivist" pedagogies. Performance assessment is particularly attractive to those science educators who conceive the subject not just as a body of knowledge to be assimilated, but also as a process of enquiry rooted in the subject matter of science, and heavily dependent on the effective use of tools and technology.

A well-designed performance task, with appropriate scoring rubrics, can elicit a rich variety of student performances, and offers the possibility of deeper understanding of cognitive processes and problem-solving strategies. For example, students asked to solve an interesting problem in a practical situation may draw on whatever content knowledge appears relevant, revealing both prior knowledge and misconceptions. The students may try several approaches, each demonstrating knowledge about different attributes of the phenomenon. The students have an opportunity to demonstrate their grasp of conceptual and procedural issues, and their reasoning ability. At the conceptual level they may do so by recognizing what data to collect, what variables to control, and how many data points they may need for an adequate picture of the phenomenon they are asked to investigate; and later, by developing explanations

[4] See for example:

Tamir, P. and Doran, R. (1992). Conclusions and Discussion of Findings Related to Practical Skills Testing in Science. *Studies in Educational Evaluation, 18* (3), pp.393-406.

Shavelson, R.J., Baxter, G.P., and Pine, J. (1991). Performance Assessment in Science. *Applied Measurement in Education, 4* (4), pp.347-362.

Haertel, E.H. and Linn, R.L. (1996). "Comparability" in G.W. Phillips (Ed.), *Technical Issues in Large-Scale Performance Assessment.* Washington, D.C.: National Center for Education Statistics.

for the trends they find in their data. Students may exhibit procedural knowledge through the use of appropriate equipment, through collecting and organizing data in tables, lists or graphs, by applying algorithms, or by reading data tables and comparing and computing differences between entries. Students may demonstrate reasoning ability by identifying trends and patterns, drawing conclusions, predicting and extrapolating to new data points, and relating findings to the original question.

Few would argue against the premise that the detailed study of student performance on practical tasks in life-like assessment situations offers greater potential for understanding student achievement than paper-and-pencil tests alone. However, in very large-scale assessments the benefits of performance assessment in terms of the extra information it may provide about student achievement must be balanced against the extra cost and complexity inherent in this mode of assessment. As the largest and most ambitious international study of student achievement in mathematics and science to date, TIMSS provided a unique environment in which to develop and implement the ideas of performance assessment within the constraints of a large-scale international comparative study.

PERFORMANCE ASSESSMENT IN TIMSS

The major challenge in developing a performance assessment for TIMSS was to identify a series of tasks in mathematics and science which could elicit a wide range of student performances, both from a subject matter perspective and from the perspective of the student behaviors necessary to complete the tasks ("performance expectations" in the terminology of TIMSS), yet which could be performed with inexpensive and readily available materials, and be adaptable to standardized administration procedures in many different cultures and languages. In addition, because the performance assessment was to be part of a much larger written assessment which made considerable demands on the time of students, teachers, and principals, it was essential that the performance assessment keep the student response burden to a minimum.

Following an extensive field-trial, a set of 13 tasks (12 for each grade level) were identified as suitable for the main assessment. These tasks could be assembled from widely-available materials, and translated readily into different languages. The issue of response burden was addressed by assigning a subset of the tasks to each student so that each student was asked to attempt only about one third of the tasks. The performance assessment was administered in a "circus" format in which a student completed three to five tasks by visiting three stations at which one or two tasks were assembled.[5] The assignment of students to stations was determined according to a predetermined scheme.

Ideally, the performance assessment would have included observations of students as they worked through the tasks, as well as evaluation of written responses. However, such observations were prohibited by cost and time constraints. Instead, structured response sheets were created with questions (items) worded to elicit evidence of specific skills and thinking processes.[6] After completing the tasks at each station, students submitted their work booklets to the performance assessment administrator, together with any products. The work recorded in the booklets and any products created during the assessment were evaluated by coders specially trained to use the TIMSS scoring rubrics.[7] The coding system developed for TIMSS allowed for the identification of common approaches and types of errors in student responses.

The TIMSS performance assessment was conducted with a subsample of fourth- and eighth-grade students that had participated in the main assessment.[8] Of the 45 countries that took part in the written assessment at the eighth grade, 21 chose also to administer the performance assessment. At the fourth grade, 10 of the 26 countries that participated in the written assessment also took part in the performance assessment. For many of these countries, this was their first experience conducting a large-scale performance assessment, and was therefore a useful model with tasks, administration procedures, and coding schemes that could help them explore the feasibility of performance assessment in their own countries.

---

[5] For more information on the performance assessment design see Appendix A of this report. See also Harmon, M. and Kelly, D.L. (1996). "Performance Assessment" in M.O. Martin and D.L. Kelly (Eds.), *Third International Mathematics and Science Study Technical Report, Volume I.* Chestnut Hill, MA: Boston College.

[6] See Baxter, G.P., Shavelson, R.J., Goldman, S.R., and Pine, J. (1992). Evaluation of Procedure-based Scoring for Hands-on Science Assessment. *Journal of Educational Measurement, 29* (1), pp. 1-17, on the use of "notebooks" as a reasonable surrogate for process observation.

[7] See Appendix A for more details on the coding procedures and reliability.

[8] See Appendix A for a more complete description of the TIMSS performance assessment sample.

THE TIMSS PERFORMANCE ASSESSMENT TASKS

Of the 13 tasks, 11 were similar in some sense across both the fourth and eighth grades. One task was unique to fourth grade, and one task to eighth grade. Each set of 12 tasks included five science tasks, five mathematics tasks, and two combination tasks, integrating mathematics and science content and skills areas. Although more than half the tasks required both science and mathematics knowledge and skills, tasks were classified according to the primary content area addressed. The tasks classified as addressing primarily science content are: Pulse, Magnets, Batteries, Rubber Band, and Solutions (eighth grade only) or Containers (fourth grade only). The mathematics tasks are Dice, Calculator, Folding and Cutting, Around the Bend, and Packaging. The two combination tasks are Shadows and Plasticine. While some tasks are identical for the fourth and eighth graders, most differ either by providing more structure for the younger students or by including additional items for the older students.

In developing the performance assessment tasks, considerable effort was expended in ensuring that the tasks would elicit a wide range of performance expectations. The term "performance expectations" is used in TIMSS to describe the cognitive or manipulative skills that students are expected to use in working on the items in a task. Performance expectations include recalling and using simple or complex information; using equipment, routine procedures, and experimental processes; problem solving; designing and conducting an investigation; analyzing and interpreting findings; formulating and justifying conclusions; and communicating scientific or mathematical information (see Table A.1 in Appendix A). Items measuring these thinking and experimental skills were distributed across all the tasks.

Each TIMSS performance assessment science task began with a primary problem or investigation to be completed by the student, followed by a series of items that required, successively, a solution to the problem, and a description of problem-solving strategies; or for the more extensive investigations, an experimental plan, data display, and students' analyses and interpretations of their own data, sometimes with predictions based on their hypotheses. In mathematics, students began with applications of routine procedures and proceeded through more complex procedures requiring data organization and analysis to creating their own problem-solving strategies, with predictions and conjectures based on their solutions.

STRUCTURE OF THE PERFORMANCE ASSESSMENT REPORT

This report describes the TIMSS performance assessment and provides a detailed summary of the performance of the students in each participating country on every item of every task. In the interests of making the results available in the shortest possible time, this report presents only descriptive summaries of student performance on the assessment tasks, and makes no attempt to relate student achievement on the performance assessment to achievement in the written assessment, or to any of the myriad background variables available in TIMSS.

Chapter 1 of this report presents a description of the tasks administered to the students in the TIMSS performance assessment, together with examples of student work and the criteria used to evaluate the work. For each task and each item within the task, results are presented for each country and for the international average. Chapter 2 displays the national differences in student achievement across all performance assessment tasks and separately for mathematics and science tasks at eighth and fourth grades. This chapter also displays results for boys and girls separately on each task for both grades. Chapter 3 displays national differences in student achievement by performance expectation at both the eighth and fourth grades. This chapter also compares the international performance of eighth-grade students on example items selected to illustrate the performance skills subcategories contained in the broader performance expectation categories.

Chapter 1

STUDENT ACHIEVEMENT ON THE
PERFORMANCE ASSESSMENT TASKS

The performance assessment tasks were chosen to sample a broad array of mathematics and science content, and to elicit from students a variety of abilities, skills, and knowledge. Each task is presented in this chapter, together with the questions (items) asked of the students, the scoring criteria applied to their responses, and a sample student response. For the majority of the tasks administered to both fourth- and eighth-grade students, the version of the task administered was different at the two grade levels. For these tasks, the full-task example with student responses is shown for the eighth-grade version, and only the modified items and scoring criteria are shown for the fourth-grade version. At both grades, the average performance of the students in each country is presented for each item, and averaged across items to provide an average task performance score for each country.

As depicted by the task averages, there is a wide range of performance across countries on each task. There is, however, also a wide range of performance across the items within each task for each country. This is a natural consequence of the way the tasks are structured, with each task containing some items that even the weakest students could attempt, as well as some quite challenging items. The variation in item difficulty within a task is a consequence also of the range of performance expectations addressed by the items, since some of those expectations make more demands on the students' abilities than others. Because of the varying difficulty of the items within each task, detailed results are presented for each item to allow a full appreciation of the performance of the students.

Although more than half the tasks require both science and mathematics knowledge and skills, each task has been classified for discussion purposes as a science or mathematics task depending on the primary content addressed. The tasks of primarily science content are Pulse, Magnets, Batteries, Rubber Band, Solutions (eighth grade only), and Containers (fourth grade only). The mathematics tasks are Dice, Calculator, Folding and Cutting, Around the Bend, and Packaging. Two tasks – Plasticine and Shadows – are referred to as "combination" tasks because they required students to integrate their mathematics and science knowledge and skills. A summary of the overall performance across tasks for each country is presented in Chapter 2.

PULSE

In the Pulse task, students were asked to find out how their pulse changed during and after exercise (5 minutes stepping up and down). They were provided with a stopwatch and a step 20-25 cm high. The task was intended to measure the ability to design and conduct an investigation (no written plan was required), that is, to collect, tabulate, analyze, and interpret data and use appropriate concepts to explain findings.

The task for eighth-grade students is shown in Figure 1.1, together with a sample student response and the criteria for a fully-correct response. Decisions about how many measurements to make, and at what intervals, were left to the individual student. Item 1 for eighth graders has two quite different aspects: the organization and representation of data in a table – a procedural skill; and the quality of the data and of the way they were collected – an aspect requiring knowledge of the content area, and of how to conduct an investigation. In common with all items involving data collection, two scores were assigned to this item – one for the quality of presentation, and the other for the quality of the data.[1] The fourth-grade version of this task did not require students to construct a data table but instead provided a practice task (Item 1) along with prepared tables (see Figure 1.2). Item 2 for fourth graders provided instructions about how often to count and record pulse beats. For these items, students' ability to organize, label, and display data in a table was not assessed, nor was the ability to decide an experimental design.

The second item for the eighth graders (Item 3 for fourth grade) required an accurate description of the trends in the data, and the third item (Item 4 for fourth grade) required conceptual knowledge of the connections among muscle work, energy needs, circulation, and heart rate in order to explain the data.

Tables 1.1 and 1.2 show the average percentage score[2] for each country on each item of the Pulse task for eighth- and fourth-grade students, respectively. The overall task average is the arithmetic mean of these average percentage scores. The 12 countries shown in the upper part of the table, in decreasing order of achievement on the overall task, were judged to have met the TIMSS requirements for testing a representative sample of students. Although all countries tried very hard to meet the TIMSS sampling requirements, several encountered difficulties in securing participation, and did not have participation rates for both schools and students of 85% (or a combined rate for the product of school and student participation of 75%) as specified in the TIMSS guidelines (i.e., Australia, England, the Netherlands, and the United States at the eighth grade). To provide a better curricular match, Colombia, Romania, and Slovenia elected to test their eighth-grade students even though these students were somewhat older than those in other countries (of these three countries, only Slovenia participated at the fourth grade). Because Hong Kong had low school participation at eighth grade, and consequently a small sample size,

[1] These two aspects of data collection, together with organization and interpretation of data, comprise what the Curriculum Frameworks call "Conducting an Investigation." For the full curriculum frameworks see Robitaille, D.F., McKnight, C.C., Schmidt, W.H., Britton, E.D., Raizen, S.A., and Nicol, C. (1993). *TIMSS Monograph No. 1: Curriculum Frameworks for Mathematics and Science.* Vancouver, B.C.: Pacific Educational Press.

[2] The percentage score on an item is the score achieved by a student expressed as a percentage of the maximum points available on that item. A country's average percentage score is the average of its students' percentage scores.

FIGURE 1.1 - PULSE FULL-TASK EXAMPLE AND SCORING CRITERIA – EIGHTH GRADE

ITEM 1

PULSE

At this station you should have

A watch with a second hand
A step on the floor to climb on

Read UNDERLINE directions carefully.

Your task:

Find out how your pulse changes when you climb up and down on a step for 5 minutes.

This is what you should do:

- Find your pulse and be sure you know how to count it. IF YOU CANNOT FIND YOUR PULSE ASK A TEACHER FOR HELP.
- Decide how often you will take measurements starting from when you are at rest.
- Climb the step for about 5 minutes and measure your pulse at regular intervals.

1. Make a table and write down the times at which you measured your pulse and the measurements you made.

Time	Pulse (beats per min)
Rest	90
1 min	110
2 min	120
3 min	125
4 min	128
5 min	125

page 1   TASK S1-P2

ITEMS 2 AND 3

2. How did your pulse change during this exercise?

My pulse became faster during this exercise. At first, it became faster quite quickly but near the end it became only a little faster with each minute until on the 5th minute it dropped a little.

3. Why do you think your pulse changed in this way?

My pulse changed this way because I was using up oxegen faster when I was exercising therefore I needed more oxegen. My heart had to pump the blood around my body faster so I would get all the oxegen I needed, as blood carries oxegen around the body.

PUT EVERYTHING BACK THE WAY YOU FOUND IT SO THAT SOMEONE ELSE CAN USE THE STATION.

TASK S1-P2   page 2

CRITERIA FOR FULLY-CORRECT RESPONSE

Item 1 - Measure pulse rates and record in table.
Response is scored for both the quality of the presentation and the quality of data collection.

Quality of presentation. i) Presents at least 2 sets of measurements in table. ii) Measurements are paired: time and number of pulse beats. iii) Labels table appropriately: data entries in columns identified by headings and/or units; units incorporated into headings or placed beside each measurement; headings or units for the number of pulse beats include the time interval.
Total Possible Points: 2

Quality of data. i) Makes at least 5 measurements (at rest, and 4 or more during exercise). ii) Pulse rates are plausible: 7 to 25 counts per 10 seconds (40-150 pulse beats per minute). iii) Pulse rate increases with exercise (may level off or slow near the end).
Total Possible Points: 3

Item 2 - Describe how pulse changes during exercise. i) Description consistent with data presented. ii) Description includes identification of the trend or pattern in the data.
Total Possible Points: 2

Item 3 - Explain why pulse changes. Includes the following three elements relating to physiological needs during exercise: i) role of muscle action (exercise results in need for more energy and oxygen in the muscles); ii) role of blood (more oxygen or food supplied by an increase in blood flow); iii) connection with heart action or pulse rate, (heart is pumping faster to supply more blood).
Total Possible Points: 3

these results are presented in Appendix B. Israel did not follow within-school sampling guidelines at the fourth grade or eighth grade and at the eighth grade it had a small sample size; its results are also presented in Appendix B. A full discussion of the sampling procedures and outcomes for each country can be found in Appendix A.

To facilitate comparisons across grades, the results for eighth and fourth grades are presented together. However, not all of the countries that tested at eighth grade also tested at fourth grade, and consequently the countries making up the international averages at eighth grade are not the same as those making up those averages at fourth grade. Comparisons across grades on the basis of the international averages should therefore be made with caution. Within individual countries, however, the relative performance between the two grades is directly comparable where the task included identical items at both grade levels.

Average country performance on the Pulse task at the eighth grade varied considerably around the international average of 44% (see Table 1.1). Despite the substantial difference between the highest- and lowest-performing countries, differences between countries with adjacent score levels may not be statistically significant because of sampling variability. Internationally, eighth-grade students had most success on the item that required them to describe the trend in their data. They found this easier than the rather straightforward task of recording and presenting their data. Explaining the causes of the changes in pulse rate observed was a challenge for most students, with relatively few students able to make the connection between muscle action, blood supply, and heart rate. Fourth-grade students were generally able to measure their pulse at rest, but found the other items demanding, particularly explaining the data.

FIGURE 1.2 - PULSE — ITEMS AND SCORING CRITERIA – FOURTH GRADE

PULSE

At this station you should have

A watch with a second hand
A step on the floor to climb on

Read <u>ALL</u> directions carefully.

Your task:

Find out how your pulse changes when you climb up and down on a step for 5 minutes.

This is what you should do:

- Find your pulse and be sure you know how to count it. IF YOU CANNOT FIND YOUR PULSE ASK A TEACHER FOR HELP.

- Count your pulse for 10 seconds.

1. Write this number of counts in the table below on the line marked 0 minutes.

2. Now climb up and down on the step for about 5 minutes. Stop after each minute and write your pulse in the table below.

Number of minutes climbing	Number of pulse counts in 10 seconds
0 Minutes	
1 Minutes	
2 Minutes	
3 Minutes	
4 Minute	
5 Minutes	

3. How did your pulse change during this exercise?

4. Why do you think your pulse changed in this way?

CRITERIA FOR FULLY-CORRECT RESPONSE

Item 1 - Measure "at rest" pulse rate and record in table. Pulse beats are plausible: 7 to 25 counts per 10 seconds (40 to 150 counts per minute).
Total Possible Points: 1

Item 2 - Measure "after exercise" pulse rates and record in table. i) Records pulse at least 4 different times during the exercise (in addition to "at rest" measurement). ii) Pulse rates are plausible: 7 to 25 counts per 10 seconds at the beginning (40 to 150 counts per minute). iii) Pulse rate increases with exercise (may level off or slow near the end).
Total Possible Points: 3

Item 3 - Describe how pulse changes during exercise. i) Description consistent with data presented. ii) Description includes identification of the trend or pattern in the data.
Total Possible Points: 2

Item 4 - Explain why pulse changes. Includes the following three elements relating to physiological needs during exercise: i) role of muscle action (exercise results in need for more energy and oxygen in the muscles); ii) role of blood (more oxygen or food supplied by an increase in blood flow); iii) connection with heart action or pulse rate, (heart is pumping faster to supply more blood).
Total Possible Points: 3

Task layout condensed for display

Table 1.1 Pulse Task: Average Percentage Score on Items – Eighth Grade*

Country	Overall Task Average▼	Average Percentage Scores on Items●			
		Item 1 Measure Pulse		Item 2 Describe Trend	Item 3 Explain Results
		Presentation	Data Quality		
		2 Points	3 Points	2 Points	3 Points
Singapore	60 (2.7)	59 (4.0)	56 (2.7)	82 (3.8)	42 (3.5)
Iran, Islamic Rep.	55 (4.5)	76 (4.8)	58 (4.8)	53 (9.0)	33 (6.6)
† Scotland	55 (2.9)	61 (3.7)	56 (3.4)	67 (4.0)	34 (3.3)
†† Switzerland	51 (1.9)	58 (3.2)	43 (3.6)	75 (3.7)	27 (3.2)
Norway	48 (1.6)	44 (2.9)	48 (3.4)	72 (2.7)	29 (3.7)
Canada	46 (2.4)	53 (3.0)	44 (3.0)	60 (3.3)	26 (2.5)
Czech Republic	46 (2.9)	45 (5.5)	38 (4.8)	72 (3.8)	27 (2.6)
Sweden	45 (2.6)	45 (3.6)	50 (2.7)	62 (4.3)	22 (4.3)
New Zealand	44 (2.0)	51 (3.5)	37 (3.0)	61 (3.2)	28 (2.6)
Spain	36 (2.1)	36 (3.0)	30 (2.7)	52 (5.3)	26 (3.0)
Cyprus	33 (2.1)	31 (3.6)	32 (3.5)	55 (3.8)	15 (1.9)
Portugal	24 (2.5)	31 (3.2)	24 (3.2)	26 (4.1)	17 (2.8)
Countries Not Satisfying Guidelines for Sample Participation Rates (See Appendix A for Details):					
Australia	54 (2.6)	68 (3.7)	46 (3.5)	71 (3.6)	31 (3.5)
² England	59 (2.2)	65 (2.4)	59 (3.6)	75 (3.0)	39 (2.7)
Netherlands	45 (2.6)	50 (4.1)	44 (3.9)	56 (3.6)	29 (2.9)
United States	50 (2.0)	54 (2.9)	43 (2.6)	72 (2.6)	33 (3.4)
Countries Not Meeting Age/Grade Specifications (See Appendix A for Details):					
Colombia	11 (1.0)	10 (1.9)	4 (1.3)	20 (3.1)	11 (2.1)
³ Romania	41 (3.6)	45 (4.5)	29 (5.1)	63 (5.7)	27 (4.1)
Slovenia	40 (3.2)	54 (3.7)	33 (5.0)	53 (4.6)	19 (3.3)
International Average	44 (0.6)	49 (0.8)	41 (0.8)	60 (1.0)	27 (0.8)

SOURCE: IEA Third International Mathematics and Science Study (TIMSS), 1994-95.

* Eighth grade in most countries; see Table 2 for information about the grades tested in each country.

● Percent of total possible points on each item averaged over students.

▼ Average of percentage scores across items; all items weighted equally.

† Met guidelines for sample participation rates only after replacement schools were included (see Appendix A for details)

1 National Desired Population does not cover all of International Desired Population (see Table A.2) - German-speaking cantons only.

2 National Defined Population covers less than 90 percent of National Desired Population for the main assessment (see Table A.2).

3 School-level exclusions for performance assessment exceed 25% of the National Desired Population (see Table A.2).

() Standard errors appear in parentheses. Because results are rounded to the nearest whole number, some totals may appear inconsistent.

Pulse Task: Average Percentage Score on Items – Fourth Grade* | Table 1.2

Country	Overall Task Average▼	Average Percentage Scores on Items•			
		Item 1 Measure Pulse at Rest	Item 2 Measure Pulse During Exercise	Item 3 Describe Trend	Item 4 Explain Results
		1 Point	3 Points	2 Points	3 Points
Iran, Islamic Rep.	41 (3.3)	77 (5.7)	44 (5.7)	32 (4.3)	9 (1.9)
Cyprus	38 (3.0)	76 (5.4)	47 (4.3)	23 (4.7)	3 (1.3)
Canada	36 (1.5)	73 (3.2)	34 (2.6)	33 (3.9)	7 (1.4)
†1 New Zealand	27 (2.1)	66 (4.7)	19 (3.2)	19 (2.5)	4 (1.2)
Portugal	22 (1.8)	61 (4.5)	23 (3.3)	5 (1.9)	1 (0.5)
Countries Not Satisfying Guidelines for Sample Participation Rates (See Appendix A for Details):					
Australia	38 (2.3)	74 (4.7)	30 (4.8)	44 (4.1)	5 (1.3)
Hong Kong	39 (2.1)	46 (4.7)	46 (4.1)	55 (3.5)	7 (1.6)
United States	42 (1.7)	77 (2.9)	32 (3.3)	48 (3.5)	9 (1.4)
Countries Not Meeting Age/Grade Specifications (See Appendix A for Details):					
Slovenia	39 (2.7)	69 (5.2)	46 (3.7)	38 (5.1)	3 (1.1)
International Average	36 (0.8)	69 (1.5)	36 (1.3)	33 (1.3)	6 (0.5)

SOURCE: IEA Third International Mathematics and Science Study (TIMSS), 1994-95.

* Fourth grade in most countries; see Table 2 for information about the grades tested in each country.

• Percent of total possible points on each item averaged over students.

▼ Average of percentage scores across items; all items weighted equally.

† Met guidelines for sample participation rates only after replacement schools were included (see Appendix A for details)

1 School-level exclusions for performance assessment exceed 25% of the National Desired Population (see Table A.3).

() Standard errors appear in parentheses. Because results are rounded to the nearest whole number, some totals may appear inconsistent.

Students performing the Magnets task were given two magnets, similar in appearance but of different magnetic strengths, and a number of magnetizable and non-magnetizable items such as steel balls, hairpins, and poker chips. The task was to conduct experiments to find which of the two magnets was the stronger, and to describe the experiments. Although on the surface the task appears to be a simple exercise in problem solving, because of its open nature it also required investigatory skills. The task was intended to measure problem solving in both strategy development and its implementation (Item 1), and the ability to support the conclusion with evidence (Item 2). Eighth-grade students were asked to experiment with the magnets and materials, without any directive as to the number or type of experiments, whereas fourth-grade students were asked to test magnets in two different the ways (see Figures 1.3 and 1.4 for descriptions of the tasks, scoring criteria for fully-correct responses, and a sample response). At either grade, only the first correct experiment was used to compute a student's score.[3]

For both grades, Item 1 was coded simply for the correctness of the solution to the problem. Students were given credit provided that they identified the correct magnet and that the test described could indeed have led to that conclusion. More than seven different approaches to the problem were recorded under Item 2, the two most popular being comparing the number of objects the magnet could hold and comparing the relative weights the magnets could lift.

Students at both grade levels found this task relatively easy. In most countries almost all eighth-grade students were able to identify the stronger magnet and to explain their strategy, and in the fourth grade the majority of students in most countries also were successful (see Tables 1.3 and 1.4). It is noteworthy that both the ability to apply a strategy to solve this problem and the ability to describe that strategy seem well developed among eighth-grade students, whereas among fourth graders there was a substantial performance difference between solving the problem and describing the strategy used for the solution.

MAGNETS

[3] Because an explicit number of tests was not required at the eighth grade, there was no penalty if students performed only one, and no extra credit if they performed several.

FIGURE 1.3 - MAGNETS FULL-TASK EXAMPLE AND SCORING CRITERIA – EIGHTH GRADE

ITEM 1

MAGNETS

At this station you should have:

6 steel balls
10 hair pins or paper clips
6 poker chips
2 steel bars
10 washers
2 magnets
A 30 cm ruler

Read ALL directions carefully.

Your task:

Use the things in the bag to find which magnet, A or B, is stronger.

This is what you should do:

- Experiment with the things in the bag to complete the sentence below.

1. I found that magnet _____B_____ is stronger.

ITEM 2

2. Describe all the different ways you used to find which magnet was stronger. You may draw pictures or diagrams as part of your answer if it helps you to explain.

What I did	What happened
	Finest tip to tip stayed together on magnet B. But on magnet A It did not.
	magnet A held less washers than magnet B.
	paper clips. at 7mm A magnet picked all of them up. At 17mm magnet B picked all of the paper clips up.

PUT ALL THE MATERIALS BACK IN THE BAG AND LEAVE THE STATION AS YOU FOUND IT.

CRITERIA FOR FULLY-CORRECT RESPONSE

Item 1 - Identify stronger magnet. Correct magnet identified according to administrator's notes.
Total Possible Points: 1

Item 2 - Describe all tests used to identify stronger magnet.
Includes at least one correct test that: i) includes description or clearly interpretable diagram; ii) shows how results of test were interpreted.
Total Possible Points: 1

FIGURE 1.4 - MAGNETS — ITEMS AND SCORING CRITERIA – FOURTH GRADE

MAGNETS

At this station you should have:

6 steel balls
10 hair pins or paper clips
6 poker chips
2 steel bars
10 washers
2 magnets
A 30 cm ruler

Read ALL directions carefully.

Your task:

Use the things in the bag to find which magnet, A or B, is stronger.

This is what you should do:

• Test the magnets in at least two different ways.

1. I found that magnet _____ is stronger.

2. Describe 2 different ways you used to find which magnet was stronger. You can draw pictures as part of your answer if it helps you to explain.

	What I did	What happened
Test One Magnet A		
Magnet B		
Test Two Magnet A		
Magnet B		

CRITERIA FOR FULLY-CORRECT RESPONSE

Item 1 - Identify stronger magnet. Correct magnet identified according to administrator's notes.
Total Possible Points: 1

Item 2 - Describe two tests used to identify stronger magnet.
 i) Records what he or she did with each magnet in both tests.
ii) Relates results of each test to the identification of the stronger magnet. (Note: Student score reflects that at least one correct test is described.)
Total Possible Points: 1

Task layout condensed for display

| Table 1.3 | Magnets Task: Average Percentage Scores on Items – Eighth Grade* |

Country	Overall Task Average▼	Average Percentage Scores on Items●	
		Item 1 Identify Stronger Magnet 1 Point	Item 2 Describe Strategy 1 Point
† Scotland	98 (0.9)	99 (0.6)	96 (1.5)
†† Switzerland	97 (1.2)	98 (1.3)	97 (1.7)
Spain	96 (1.4)	97 (1.5)	96 (1.9)
Sweden	95 (1.6)	95 (1.7)	95 (2.2)
Singapore	95 (0.9)	98 (1.0)	92 (1.7)
Portugal	94 (1.6)	97 (1.4)	90 (2.4)
New Zealand	93 (1.6)	92 (1.6)	94 (1.9)
Canada	92 (1.5)	95 (1.6)	89 (2.4)
Norway	91 (2.0)	88 (3.0)	94 (2.3)
Czech Republic	86 (2.3)	86 (3.3)	86 (2.2)
Cyprus	86 (2.3)	93 (1.9)	78 (3.5)
Iran, Islamic Rep.	45 (4.9)	52 (8.0)	39 (5.6)
Countries Not Satisfying Guidelines for Sample Participation Rates (See Appendix A for Details):			
Australia	92 (1.4)	97 (1.2)	86 (2.1)
² England	99 (0.6)	99 (0.9)	99 (0.7)
Netherlands	94 (2.1)	96 (1.9)	93 (2.6)
United States	85 (2.5)	90 (2.6)	81 (3.4)
Countries Not Meeting Age/Grade Specifications (See Appendix A for Details):			
Colombia	96 (1.3)	96 (1.7)	95 (1.8)
³ Romania	83 (3.5)	78 (5.2)	89 (3.6)
Slovenia	92 (1.9)	94 (2.1)	91 (2.1)
International Average	90 (0.5)	92 (0.6)	88 (0.6)

SOURCE: IEA Third International Mathematics and Science Study (TIMSS), 1994-95.

* Eighth grade in most countries; see Table 2 for information about the grades tested in each country.

● Percent of total possible points on each item averaged over students.

▼ Average of percentage scores across items; all items weighted equally.

† Met guidelines for sample participation rates only after replacement schools were included (see Appendix A for details)

1 National Desired Population does not cover all of International Desired Population (see Table A.2) - German-speaking cantons only.

2 National Defined Population covers less than 90 percent of National Desired Population for the main assessment (see Table A.2).

3 School-level exclusions for performance assessment exceed 25% of the National Desired Population (see Table A.2).

() Standard errors appear in parentheses. Because results are rounded to the nearest whole number, some totals may appear inconsistent.

Magnets Task: Average Percentage Score on Items – Fourth Grade* Table 1.4

Country	Overall Task Average▼	Average Percentage Scores on Items●	
		Item 1 Identify Stronger Magnet 1 Point	**Item 2** Describe Strategy 1 Point
Canada	84 (2.3)	92 (2.1)	76 (3.1)
†† New Zealand	84 (2.2)	86 (2.3)	83 (2.9)
Portugal	74 (3.1)	83 (3.3)	65 (4.2)
Cyprus	68 (3.9)	82 (4.1)	54 (4.6)
Iran, Islamic Rep.	42 (5.1)	49 (5.2)	35 (6.1)
Countries Not Satisfying Guidelines for Sample Participation Rates (See Appendix A for Details):			
Australia	77 (3.1)	80 (3.8)	74 (3.6)
Hong Kong	74 (3.8)	82 (3.9)	65 (5.5)
United States	73 (3.0)	82 (3.2)	65 (4.2)
Countries Not Meeting Age/Grade Specifications (See Appendix A for Details):			
Slovenia	74 (3.8)	84 (3.8)	63 (4.6)
International Average	72 (1.2)	80 (1.2)	64 (1.5)

SOURCE: IEA Third International Mathematics and Science Study (TIMSS), 1994-95.

* Fourth grade in most countries; see Table 2 for information about the grades tested in each country.

● Percent of total possible points on each item averaged over students.

▼ Average of percentage scores across items; all items weighted equally.

† Met guidelines for sample participation rates only after replacement schools were included (see Appendix A for details)

[1] School-level exclusions for performance assessment exceed 25% of the National Desired Population (see Table A.3).

() Standard errors appear in parentheses. Because results are rounded to the nearest whole number, some totals may appear inconsistent.

In the Batteries task, students were provided with four unmarked batteries and a flashlight. To begin, they were asked to find out which of the batteries were good and which were worn out. The task was intended to measure students' ability to develop and implement problem-solving strategies and use experimental evidence to support a conclusion, but it also sampled specific knowledge about electricity to solve a routine problem and to develop a concept-based explanation for the solution. Item 1 required students to identify the good batteries, which could be achieved by a systematic process of trial and error. Item 2 called for a description of the strategy used to identify the good batteries. Item 3 in this task required selection of the correct arrangement of batteries in a flashlight. Item 4 asked students to explain why their solution was correct, which requires knowledge of the concept of a complete circuit and an understanding of the direction of flow of electrical current.

Scoring criteria and a sample response for the Batteries task are presented in Figure 1.5. This task was exactly the same for eighth- and fourth-grade students.

Eighth-grade students in most countries had no difficulty in identifying the correct alignment of batteries in the flashlight (see Table 1.5, Item 3 – average percentage score: 91%), and were well able to identify the good batteries (Item 1 – average percentage score: 74%). They were somewhat less successful in describing the strategy used to identify the good batteries (Item 2 – average percentage score: 59%), and in explaining why their choice of battery alignment was the best one (Item 4 – average percentage score: 42%). Fourth-grade students also did quite well in identifying the correct battery alignment (see Table 1.6, Item 3 – average percentage score: 72%) and moderately well in finding the good batteries (Item 1 – average percentage score: 51%), but found describing their strategy (Item 2 – average percentage score: 23%) and explaining their choice (Item 4 – average percentage score: 19%) much more difficult.

The most typical partial-credit responses stated that the "positive pole must touch the negative" (without mentioning the reason), or "I tried all the combinations one after the other and this is what I got." A number of students merely repeated their strategy descriptions, perhaps not understanding the difference between describing what happened and explaining why it happened.

BATTERIES

FIGURE 1.5 - BATTERIES FULL-TASK EXAMPLE AND SCORING CRITERIA – EIGHTH AND FOURTH GRADES

ITEMS 1 AND 2

BATTERIES

At this station you should have:

A flashlight (or torch)
Four batteries in a plastic bag: Batteries A, B, C, D

Read ALL directions carefully.

Your task:

Find out which of the batteries are good and which are worn-out.

This is what you should do:

- Think about how you could solve this problem.
- Then work out which batteries are good and which are worn-out.

1. Based on your investigation which of the batteries are good and which are worn-out? Write the letters of the batteries in the spaces below.

   Good batteries ___A D___

   Worn-out batteries ___BC___

2. Write down how you decided which batteries were worn-out.

   I put different batteries together and switch the Torch on. The combinations I used were
   CD¹ AB² DB³ CA⁴ AD⁵ CB⁶ and A and D batteries together were the brightest so A and D are the got batteries and BC are the worn-out ones.

TASK S3-P2

ITEMS 3 AND 4

3. How should the batteries be put in the flashlight to give the brightest light? Here are 3 different ways of putting the batteries in the flashlight. Draw a circle around the picture that you think shows the correct way.

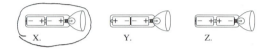

   X.   Y.   Z.

4. Why is the way you chose the best way to put in the batteries?

   Because electricity flows in a circle or circuit. and to get a circuit with batteries the pole have to be the opposite of each other like a magnet, and to complete the circuit the top and bottom poles have to be joint with a electrical conducting metal

CRITERIA FOR FULLY-CORRECT RESPONSE

Item 1 - Identify which batteries are good and which are worn out.
All batteries correctly identified (per administrator notes).
Total Possible Points: 2

Item 2 - Describe how worn-out batteries were identified.
i) Shows evidence of systematic and definitive testing of different combinations of batteries. ii) "Systematic" is evidenced by trying all combinations of batteries or trying selected combinations using reasoning and scientific knowledge to eliminate some trials.
Total Possible Points: 2

Item 3 - Identify which arrangement of batteries inside flashlight will produce the brightest light. Correct arrangement identified (X).
Total Possible Points: 1

Item 4 - Explain why chosen arrangement is the best one.
i) Identifies correct arrangement. ii) Includes concepts of complete circuit and/or current flowing in one direction.
Total Possible Points: 2

Table 1.5 — Batteries Task: Average Percentage Score on Items – Eighth Grade*

Country	Overall Task Average▼	Average Percentage Scores on Items●			
		Item 1 Identify Good/Bad Batteries 2 Points	Item 2 Describe Tests 2 Points	Item 3 Identify Arrangement 1 Points	Item 4 Explain Arrangement 2 Points
Singapore	79 (2.1)	83 (3.4)	72 (3.7)	98 (1.4)	63 (2.7)
†† Switzerland	75 (2.1)	87 (3.3)	77 (3.7)	94 (2.2)	41 (3.1)
Spain	73 (1.7)	84 (3.0)	75 (3.6)	93 (2.2)	41 (2.3)
Sweden	71 (2.9)	77 (3.7)	61 (4.5)	90 (2.7)	57 (4.3)
† Scotland	68 (2.4)	72 (4.1)	59 (3.5)	94 (2.1)	47 (3.2)
New Zealand	68 (1.6)	78 (3.0)	49 (3.0)	97 (1.2)	47 (2.1)
Norway	67 (1.7)	92 (2.1)	56 (3.6)	91 (2.4)	29 (2.3)
Czech Republic	66 (2.8)	76 (4.2)	63 (4.3)	87 (4.3)	39 (2.7)
Cyprus	66 (2.2)	81 (4.1)	72 (3.3)	87 (3.1)	25 (2.6)
Canada	62 (2.1)	66 (3.4)	52 (4.0)	92 (1.8)	38 (1.5)
Iran, Islamic Rep.	52 (4.0)	78 (5.0)	52 (7.7)	64 (3.5)	15 (3.0)
Portugal	50 (2.2)	39 (4.3)	29 (4.1)	92 (2.1)	41 (2.4)
Countries Not Satisfying Guidelines for Sample Participation Rates (See Appendix A for Details):					
Australia	71 (1.8)	81 (2.4)	71 (3.5)	93 (3.1)	40 (2.5)
² England	77 (2.0)	89 (2.7)	71 (3.3)	91 (2.3)	56 (3.2)
Netherlands	63 (2.9)	68 (3.4)	42 (5.8)	93 (1.7)	47 (3.4)
United States	56 (1.9)	59 (4.1)	35 (3.7)	97 (1.1)	34 (2.3)
Countries Not Meeting Age/Grade Specifications (See Appendix A for Details):					
Colombia	55 (2.2)	61 (5.5)	39 (4.0)	80 (5.5)	40 (3.8)
³ Romania	75 (2.2)	73 (4.4)	75 (4.3)	96 (1.6)	56 (3.2)
Slovenia	71 (1.8)	69 (3.4)	64 (3.3)	97 (1.4)	52 (3.0)
International Average	67 (0.5)	74 (0.9)	59 (1.0)	91 (0.6)	42 (0.7)

SOURCE: IEA Third International Mathematics and Science Study (TIMSS), 1994-95.

* Eighth grade in most countries; see Table 2 for information about the grades tested in each country.

● Percent of total possible points on each item averaged over students.

▼ Average of percentage scores across items; all items weighted equally.

† Met guidelines for sample participation rates only after replacement schools were included (see Appendix A for details)

¹ National Desired Population does not cover all of International Desired Population (see Table A.2) - German-speaking cantons only.

² National Defined Population covers less than 90 percent of National Desired Population for the main assessment (see Table A.2).

³ School-level exclusions for performance assessment exceed 25% of the National Desired Population (see Table A.2).

() Standard errors appear in parentheses. Because results are rounded to the nearest whole number, some totals may appear inconsistent.

Batteries Task: Average Percentage Score on Items – Fourth Grade* | Table 1.6

Country	Overall Task Average▼	Average Percentage Scores on Items●			
		Item 1 Identify Good/Bad Batteries 2 Points	Item 2 Describe Tests 2 Points	Item 3 Identify Arrangement 1 Points	Item 4 Explain Arrangement 2 Points
Canada	48 (2.0)	60 (3.7)	27 (2.6)	82 (3.0)	23 (2.2)
Cyprus	41 (2.2)	66 (5.0)	27 (3.9)	61 (3.5)	11 (2.1)
Iran, Islamic Rep.	40 (3.2)	73 (4.2)	27 (4.4)	48 (5.5)	13 (2.6)
†1 New Zealand	37 (1.4)	38 (3.7)	8 (1.5)	80 (2.6)	21 (2.2)
Portugal	31 (2.5)	32 (5.3)	11 (2.5)	62 (5.2)	19 (2.1)
Countries Not Satisfying Guidelines for Sample Participation Rates (See Appendix A for Details):					
Australia	40 (1.9)	48 (5.2)	25 (2.7)	71 (4.4)	17 (1.9)
Hong Kong	42 (2.0)	49 (5.0)	17 (3.1)	88 (2.9)	15 (3.5)
United States	38 (2.2)	38 (3.4)	21 (3.4)	76 (3.0)	19 (1.7)
Countries Not Meeting Age/Grade Specifications (See Appendix A for Details):					
Slovenia	54 (2.0)	58 (4.4)	44 (2.6)	83 (2.7)	30 (3.0)
International Average	41 (0.7)	51 (1.5)	23 (1.0)	72 (1.3)	19 (0.8)

SOURCE: IEA Third International Mathematics and Science Study (TIMSS), 1994-95.

* Fourth grade in most countries; see Table 2 for information about the grades tested in each country.

● Percent of total possible points on each item averaged over students.

▼ Average of percentage scores across items; all items weighted equally.

† Met guidelines for sample participation rates only after replacement schools were included (see Appendix A for details)

1 School-level exclusions for performance assessment exceed 25% of the National Desired Population (see Table A.3).

() Standard errors appear in parentheses. Because results are rounded to the nearest whole number, some totals may appear inconsistent.

The Rubber Band task asked students to investigate what would happen to the length of a rubber band as more and more rings were hung on it. They were provided with an experimental set-up that included a clipboard with a sheet of white paper and a length of rubber band suspended from the clip. A paper clip bent into the shape of a hook was attached to the other end of the rubber band, and students were given a set of metal rings to be hung onto the hook as weights (see Figures 1.6 and 1.7).

The instructions were to add weights to the band one at a time and record the length of the rubber band each time. The task was intended as an investigation into elasticity, with specific items within the task assessing particular skills, i.e., the ability to follow a procedure and measure and record data accurately (Item 1); to make a graph of the data (Item 2 – eighth-grade students only); to extract information from a table or graph students have constructed (Item 3 for eighth grade, Item 2 for fourth grade); to describe a trend in the data they have recorded (Item 4 for eighth grade, Item 3 for fourth grade); to extrapolate beyond the data they have recorded (Item 5 for eighth grade, Item 4 for fourth grade); and to explain the trend in the data that justified the extrapolation (Item 6 – eighth grade only).

Fourth-grade students were provided with a table and explicit instructions on how to collect and record data, whereas eighth-grade students had to construct and label the table themselves. Therefore, the quality of the data organization was not assessed for fourth graders, nor were fourth graders required to graph their data. Criteria for a fully-correct response to each item and a sample response are provided in Figures 1.6 and 1.7.

Eighth-grade students found the data collection and display easy in this task, probably due to the prescriptive directions that guided them step by step in what and how to measure and record (Table 1.7, Item 1 – average percentage scores: 85% and 88%). However, graphing the resulting data (Item 2 – average percentage score: 50%) proved more difficult. Calculating the increase in length, which required a combination of two routine procedures – reading the data table and computing a designated difference – was also difficult (Item 3 – average percentage score: 47%). Eighth-grade students were generally able to describe the trend in their data (Item 4 – average percentage score: 64%) and make an extrapolation on the basis of that trend (Item 5 – average percentage score: 59%), but were less successful in explaining the trend and justifying their extrapolation (Item 6 – average percentage score: 49%).

Fourth-grade students were very successful in measuring and recording the data from the task (Table 1.8, Item 1 – average percentage score: 84%), and in some countries could extrapolate from their data quite well (Item 4 – average percentage score: 50%), but generally found the other items very difficult.

RUBBER BAND

FIGURE 1.6 - RUBBER BAND FULL-TASK EXAMPLE AND SCORING CRITERIA – EIGHTH GRADE

INTRODUCTION TO TASK

RUBBER BAND

At this station you should have:

A clipboard with a rubber band
A large paper clip attached to one end of the rubber band
Metal rings to hang on the large paper clip
A 30 cm ruler
Some sheets of plain paper.
2 sheets of graph or squared paper

Read ALL directions carefully.

Your task:

Find out how the length of the rubber band changes as more and more rings are hung on it.

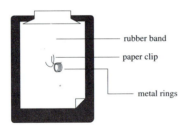

rubber band
paper clip
metal rings

This is what you should do:

• Hang the metal rings onto the paper clip one by one

• Measure the length for each new ring.

• Record your measurements in the table.

ITEMS 1, 2, 3, AND 4

1. Write your measurements in the table. Remember to write a heading for each column.

Number of Rings	Length in cm
1	17.5
2	18.0
3	18.5
4	19.0
5	19.5
6	20.0
7	20.5
8	21.0
9	21.5
10	22.0

2. Graph your results on the paper provided. You may use a graph or a bar chart.

ANSWER QUESTIONS 3 TO 6, USING YOUR TABLE, GRAPH, OR BAR CHART.

3. When there are 2 rings on the paper clip and 3 more are then added, how much longer does the rubber band become?

The rubber band becomes _____ 1.5 _____ cm longer.

4. Describe how the rubber band changed in length as more and more rings were added.

Each time I added a ring the length became 0.5 of a cm longer

Please turn the page.

ITEM 2 RESPONSE

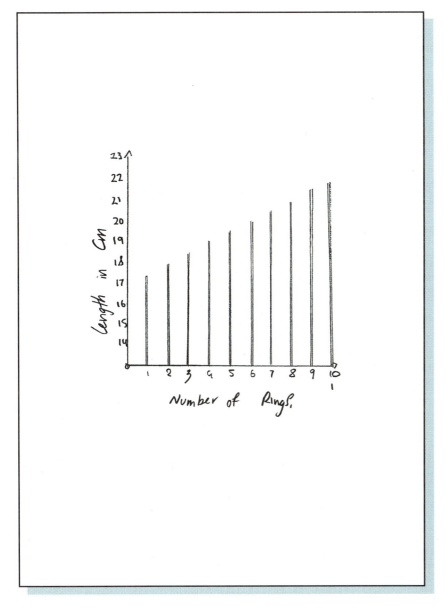

ITEMS 5 AND 6

5. What do you think would be the length of the rubber band if you could add 2 more rings than you have been given?

I think the total length of the rubber band might be __23__ cm.

6. Why do you think this would happen? *This would happen because for every Ring put on the length becomes 0.5 of a centimeter longer.*

PUT EVERYTHING BACK THE WAY YOU FOUND IT SO THAT SOMEONE ELSE CAN USE THE STATION.

FIGURE 1.6 (CONT.) RUBBER BAND – EIGHTH GRADE

CRITERIA FOR FULLY-CORRECT RESPONSE

Item 1 - Record rubber band length as rings are added. Response is scored for both the quality of the presentation and the quality of data collection.

Quality of presentation. i) Presents at least 2 sets of measurements in table. ii) Measurements are paired: number of rings and length of rubber band. iii) Labels table appropriately: data entries in columns identified by headings and/or units; units incorporated into headings or placed beside each measurement.
Total Possible Points: 2

Quality of data. i) Records length of rubber band for five or more different numbers of rings. ii) Shows reasonable trend in data: rubber band length increases with number of rings (at least for first few measurements); length *may* increase steadily at first and then stabilize or level off; elastic limit of rubber band *may* be exceeded and measurements toward the end show very large or erratic increases.
Total Possible Points: 3

Item 2 - Graph results (graph or bar chart). i) Axes correctly scaled. ii) Axes correctly labeled, including units where appropriate. iii) Measurements recorded in graph are consistent with data table. iv) Graph reflects trend in data.
Total Possible Points: 3

Item 3 - Calculate increase in length of rubber band when rings are added. i) Records amounts consistent with data in table, graph, or bar chart. ii) Calculates increase correctly.
Total Possible Points: 2

Item 4 - Describe how rubber band length changes as more rings are added. i) Description corresponds to data in table or graph. ii) Identifies trend in data. Trend may show that rubber band length increases consistently with each added ring; initially rubber band length increases consistently, then begins to level off; increases become larger or erratic with more rings (elastic limit of band exceeded); no change in length occurs (rubber band too strong for weights, per administrator notes).
Total Possible Points: 2

Item 5 - Predict increase in length of rubber band. Makes reasonable prediction, based on the data presented in the table or graph.
Total Possible Points: 1

Item 6 - Explain reason for prediction. i) Refers to the increase in length as read from the table or extrapolated from graph. ii) Attempts to relate weight or number of rings to elasticity of the rubber band. iii) Response is consistent with data in table or graph.
Total Possible Points:2

FIGURE 1.7 - RUBBER BAND
ITEMS AND SCORING CRITERIA – FOURTH GRADE

RUBBER BAND

At this station you should have:

A board with a rubber band
A paper clip attached to one end of the rubber band
Metal rings to hang on the paper clip
A 30 cm ruler
Some sheets of plain paper

Read ALL directions carefully.

> **Your task:**
>
> Find out how the length of the rubber band changes as more and more rings are hung on it.

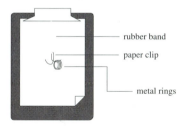

rubber band

paper clip

metal rings

This is what you should do:

- Measure the length of the rubber band and write it in the table on the line marked "0 - rubber band with no ring."

- Hang one ring on the paper clip and measure the new length of the rubber band. Write it in the table opposite "1 ring."

- Keep adding rings one by one. Measure each new length and write it in the table.

1. **Table of Measurements**

NUMBER OF MASSES	LENGTH OF RUBBER BAND (in centimeters)
0 - rubber band with no ring	
1 ring	
2 rings	
3 rings	
4 rings	
5 rings	
6 rings	
7 rings	
8 rings	
9 rings	
10 rings	

USE YOUR TABLE TO ANSWER QUESTIONS 2 TO 5.

2. When there are 2 rings on the paper clip and 3 more are then added, how much longer does the rubber band become?

   The rubber band becomes _____ cm longer.

3. How did the rubber band change in length as more and more rings were added?

4. What do you think the length of the rubber band would be if you could add 2 more rings than you have been given?

   I think the total length of the rubber band might be _____ cm.

5. Why do you think this would happen?

FIGURE 1.7 (CONT.) RUBBER BAND – FOURTH GRADE

CRITERIA FOR FULLY-CORRECT RESPONSE

Item 1 - Record rubber band length as rings are hung from it.
i) Records length of rubber band for at least five different numbers of rings. ii) Shows reasonable trend in data: rubber band lengths increase with numbers of rings (at least for first few sets of measurements); length *may* increase steadily at first, and then stabilize or level off; elastic limit of rubber band *may* be exceeded and measurements toward the end show very large or erratic increases.
Total Possible Points: 3

Item 2 - Calculate increase in length of rubber band when rings are added. i) Records amounts consistent with data in table.
ii) Calculates increase correctly.
Total Possible Points: 2

Item 3 - Describe how rubber band length changes as more rings are added. i) Description corresponds to data in table or graph.
ii) Identifies trend in data. Trend may show that rubber band length increases consistently with each added ring; initially rubber band length increases consistently, then begins to level off; increases become larger or erratic with more rings (elastic limit of band exceeded); no change in length occurs (rubber band too strong for weights, per administrator notes).
Total Possible Points: 2

Item 4 - Predict increase in length of rubber band. Makes reasonable prediction, based on the data presented in the table.
Total Possible Points: 1

Item 5- Explain reason for prediction. i) Refers to the increase in length as read from the table. ii) Attempts to relate weight or number of rings to elasticity of the rubber band. iii) Response is consistent with data in table.
Total Possible Points:2

Rubber Band Task: Average Percentage Score on Items - Eighth Grade* | Table 1.7

Country	Overall Task Average▼	Average Percentage Scores on Items ●						
		Item 1 Measure Lengths		Item 2 Graph Results	Item 3 Calculate Increase	Item 4 Describe Trend	Item 5 Predict Length	Item 6 Explain Prediction
		Presentation	Data Quality					
		2 Points	3 Points	3 Points	2 Points	2 Points	1 Points	2 Points
Singapore	80 (1.5)	95 (1.3)	99 (0.7)	67 (2.3)	67 (4.2)	87 (1.7)	84 (3.0)	61 (2.3)
† Scotland	75 (1.8)	95 (1.7)	96 (1.6)	69 (2.8)	57 (3.7)	73 (2.6)	78 (4.2)	54 (3.8)
Canada	71 (2.0)	87 (2.0)	95 (1.4)	66 (3.2)	55 (6.1)	59 (3.9)	73 (3.1)	59 (3.2)
Sweden	70 (2.4)	83 (2.8)	93 (1.8)	55 (3.4)	64 (3.8)	65 (4.6)	72 (4.1)	59 (4.3)
†† Switzerland	67 (1.9)	93 (2.2)	93 (1.9)	31 (4.2)	58 (5.0)	73 (3.4)	68 (4.5)	53 (4.4)
New Zealand	65 (1.8)	89 (1.8)	93 (1.4)	67 (3.1)	56 (3.6)	68 (2.8)	51 (3.4)	33 (2.8)
Czech Republic	65 (3.6)	81 (2.3)	86 (2.6)	44 (4.1)	54 (5.8)	70 (4.3)	66 (6.6)	54 (5.9)
Norway	63 (1.9)	80 (2.6)	96 (1.2)	49 (3.1)	56 (3.8)	60 (4.0)	53 (4.1)	46 (3.7)
Cyprus	59 (2.3)	83 (3.1)	87 (2.9)	41 (4.4)	46 (5.2)	53 (3.7)	58 (3.7)	46 (4.7)
Iran, Islamic Rep.	56 (5.4)	83 (5.4)	80 (6.4)	26 (6.5)	20 (5.2)	62 (4.1)	56 (8.6)	63 (8.9)
Spain	51 (2.0)	68 (3.3)	75 (3.0)	33 (3.3)	33 (4.0)	58 (3.9)	44 (4.4)	48 (2.6)
Portugal	51 (2.3)	78 (3.0)	83 (3.5)	41 (3.4)	32 (3.8)	44 (4.2)	47 (4.6)	34 (4.5)
Countries Not Satisfying Guidelines for Sample Participation Rates (See Appendix A for Details):								
Australia	64 (2.4)	92 (2.2)	92 (1.8)	55 (3.1)	49 (4.1)	65 (5.1)	57 (4.3)	41 (4.1)
² England	79 (1.4)	95 (1.5)	98 (0.9)	76 (2.4)	55 (3.3)	84 (2.9)	80 (3.1)	68 (3.6)
Netherlands	70 (1.9)	89 (2.1)	95 (1.3)	71 (2.9)	62 (3.5)	63 (4.0)	53 (5.8)	61 (3.8)
United States	63 (2.4)	83 (3.1)	88 (2.3)	54 (3.6)	45 (4.1)	68 (3.2)	59 (4.0)	41 (3.1)
Countries Not Meeting Age/Grade Specifications (See Appendix A for Details):								
Colombia	40 (3.7)	58 (7.4)	67 (5.8)	14 (3.0)	17 (3.9)	55 (5.4)	28 (4.3)	39 (3.9)
³ Romania	45 (3.0)	87 (3.1)	60 (4.1)	39 (4.2)	26 (5.4)	47 (3.0)	30 (4.8)	25 (3.6)
Slovenia	64 (1.7)	93 (1.6)	91 (1.8)	58 (3.3)	35 (4.1)	57 (3.6)	65 (5.1)	47 (3.8)
International Average	63 (0.6)	85 (0.7)	88 (0.7)	50 (0.8)	47 (1.0)	64 (0.9)	59 (1.1)	49 (1.0)

SOURCE: IEA Third International Mathematics and Science Study (TIMSS), 1994-95.

* Eighth grade in most countries; see Table 2 for information about the grades tested in each country.

● Percent of total possible points on each item averaged over students.

▼ Average of percentage scores across items; all items weighted equally.

† Met guidelines for sample participation rates only after replacement schools were included (see Appendix A for details)

¹ National Desired Population does not cover all of International Desired Population (see Table A.2) - German-speaking cantons only.

² National Defined Population covers less than 90 percent of National Desired Population for the main assessment (see Table A.2).

³ School-level exclusions for performance assessment exceed 25% of the National Desired Population (see Table A.2).

() Standard errors appear in parentheses. Because results are rounded to the nearest whole number, some totals may appear inconsistent.

Table 1.8 Rubber Band Task: Average Percentage Score on Items – Fourth Grade*

Country	Overall Task Average▼	Average Percentage Scores on Items●				
		Item 1 Record Lengths 3 Points	Item 2 Calculate Increase 2 Points	Item 3 Describe Trend 2 Points	Item 4 Predict Length 1 Point	Item 5 Explain Prediction 2 Points
Canada	55 (1.5)	96 (0.8)	23 (2.5)	49 (2.6)	69 (2.6)	39 (2.6)
Cyprus	45 (3.2)	89 (3.2)	26 (4.0)	41 (3.0)	44 (5.0)	26 (4.1)
†1 New Zealand	44 (2.3)	89 (2.9)	27 (3.2)	36 (2.9)	53 (3.4)	13 (2.8)
Iran, Islamic Rep.	36 (3.3)	76 (4.8)	13 (2.6)	36 (2.8)	31 (6.3)	26 (4.4)
Portugal	27 (2.2)	55 (4.4)	16 (3.3)	23 (2.9)	25 (3.5)	15 (2.9)
Countries Not Satisfying Guidelines for Sample Participation Rates (See Appendix A for Details):						
Australia	52 (2.9)	84 (2.7)	30 (3.4)	41 (5.4)	71 (5.3)	33 (2.7)
Hong Kong	43 (2.5)	91 (2.5)	26 (4.2)	43 (2.9)	37 (5.4)	18 (3.4)
United States	45 (1.8)	77 (1.9)	30 (3.5)	41 (3.0)	54 (3.4)	22 (2.5)
Countries Not Meeting Age/Grade Specifications (See Appendix A for Details):						
Slovenia	51 (1.7)	96 (1.5)	20 (3.5)	43 (2.5)	64 (4.6)	34 (3.1)
International Average	44 (0.8)	84 (1.0)	23 (1.1)	39 (1.1)	50 (1.5)	25 (1.1)

SOURCE: IEA Third International Mathematics and Science Study (TIMSS), 1994-95.

* Fourth grade in most countries; see Table 2 for information about the grades tested in each country.

● Percent of total possible points on each item averaged over students.

▼ Average of percentage scores across items; all items weighted equally.

† Met guidelines for sample participation rates only after replacement schools were included (see Appendix A for details)

1 School-level exclusions for performance assessment exceed 25% of the National Desired Population (see Table A.3).

() Standard errors appear in parentheses. Because results are rounded to the nearest whole number, some totals may appear inconsistent.

In the Solutions task, students were asked to investigate the effect of temperature on the speed with which tablets dissolved in water. The students were provided with several beakers, a supply of hot and cold water, tablets that would fizz as they dissolved, a stirrer, a thermometer, a 30cm ruler, and a stopwatch or wall clock with a second hand. This task was intended to measure students' ability to plan an investigation; use a thermometer correctly and accurately; collect, tabulate, analyze, and interpret data; invoke concept knowledge to explain findings; and evaluate the entire investigation. This task was administered to eighth-grade students only.

Unique among all items in the performance assessment, the last item of this task was intended to measure students' ability to evaluate the experiment by identifying the need and reasons for changes. Possible changes could be in design, materials, method, use of equipment, number of repeated measurements, or they could be intended to verify that the variables ignored were indeed irrelevant. Full credit was awarded only if the reasons for the changes were included. A description of the task, along with a sample response and scoring criteria for a fully-correct response for each item, are presented in Figure 1.8.

Students internationally found it somewhat difficult to describe their plan for the investigation in writing (Table 1.9, Item 1 – average percentage score: 44%). Carrying out the measurements, recording, and presenting the data were generally easier (Item 2 – average percentage scores: 62% and 59%). Students did best at providing conclusions consistent with their data (Item 3 – average percentage score: 77%). Presenting an explanation for the observed phenomena was much more difficult (Item 4 – average percentage score: 22%). To receive full credit, the explanation needed to demonstrate knowledge both of the relationship between higher temperature and greater energy and of the effect of this energy on the dissolving process.

Students also found it difficult to evaluate their plan and describe modifications they would make (Item 5 – average percentage score: 30%). Almost half of the students claimed, erroneously, that no changes were needed in their original plans. On the other hand, about one quarter of the students internationally stated, correctly, "no change required," i.e., their original plan was found to be complete and correct. To be able to evaluate one's work – design, data collection, and results – is a sophisticated form of scientific thinking, and one that many eighth-grade students in these countries have yet to acquire.

SOLUTIONS

FIGURE 1.8 - SOLUTIONS FULL-TASK EXAMPLE AND SCORING CRITERIA – EIGHTH GRADE

ITEM 1

SOLUTIONS

At this station you should have:

Hot and cold water
Several beakers
Some tablets
A stirrer
A clock or watch with a second hand
A thermometer
A 30 cm ruler

Read ALL directions carefully.

> **Your task:**
>
> Investigate what effect different water temperatures have on the speed with which the tablet dissolves.

This is what you should do:

- Plan an experiment to find out what effect different water temperatures have on the speed with which the tablet dissolves.

1. Write your plan here. Your plan should include
   - what you will measure.
   - how many measurements you will make.
   - how you will present your measurements in a table.

Take a measurement of the time it takes for the tablet to completely dissolve in 200ml
Take 1 measurement in cold, one in hot and one in warm (½ cold, ½ hot).
Make a table with time it takes for each ~~if~~ to dissolve in each temperature

page 1   TASK S5-P2

ITEMS 2 AND 3

2. Carry out your tests on the tablets. Make a table and record all your measurements.

Temperature °C	time (s)
Cold 13°C	62
30 Warm 42°C	32
Hot 79°C	30
1 part Hot - 3 part cold 28°C	41
1 part cold - 3 part hot 54°C	30

3. According to your investigation, what effect do different water temperatures have on the speed with which a tablet dissolves?

In higher water temperatures the tablets dissolve faster and more thoroughly than cold water

Please turn the page.

TASK S5-P2   page 2

44

ITEMS 4 AND 5

4. Explain why you think different water temperatures have this effect.

In hotter water the particles have more energy. When the tablet is dropped in the energy breaks apart the tablet and dissolves it. The more energy, or the hotter it is, the faster this happens.

5. If you had to change your plan, describe the changes you made and why you made them. If you did not have to change your plan, write "No change."

Hot and warm were very similar. I try a test between warm and cold and between warm and hot. I found that the time it takes is similar above approx 50°C. Maybe there is a minimum time for the tablet to dissolve.

EMPTY YOUR BEAKERS INTO THE WASTE CONTAINER, DRY THEM, AND LEAVE EVERYTHING THE WAY YOU FOUND IT.

page 3   TASK S5-P2

CRITERIA FOR FULLY-CORRECT RESPONSE

Item 1 - Plan investigation . i) Describes how the investigation will be conducted. ii) States what variables will be measured or observed; includes both solution time and temperature. iii) Provides control for other variables, or renders other variables irrelevant by design.
Total Possible Points: 2

Item 2 - Conduct investigation and record measurements in table. Response is scored for both the quality of the presentation and the quality of the data collection.

Quality of presentation. i) Presents at least 2 sets of measurements in table. ii) Measurements are paired: dissolution time and temperature. iii) Labels table appropriately: data entries in columns identified by headings and/or units; units incorporated into headings or placed beside each measurement.
Total Possible Points: 2

Quality of data. i) Records solution time for at least three temperature points. ii) Measurements are plausible: time and temperature (10° to 100° C) iii) Records solution times that decline as temperature increases.
Total Possible Points: 3

Item 3 - Draw conclusions about effect of temperature.
i) Conclusion is consistent with data table or other presentation of data (graph or text). ii) Describes <u>relationship</u> presented in the data.
Total Possible Points: 2

Item 4 - Explain conclusions. i) Relates higher temperature to greater energy or speed of particles (atoms, molecules, etc.). ii) Makes connection between greater speed or energy of water molecules and the effect on the tablet (may be implicit).
Total Possible Points: 2

Item 5 - Evaluate design and experiment; describe changes.
i) Response is consistent with the way student recorded and described data ("no change" is acceptable if student plan was complete).
ii) Changes may be made in method, use of equipment, number of measurements taken, etc; reason for change must be included.
Total Possible Points:2

Table 1.9 Solutions Task: Average Percentage Score on Items - Eighth Grade*

Country	Overall Task Average▼	Average Percentage Scores on Items•					
		Item 1 Plan Investigation	Item 2 Conduct Investigation		Item 3 Draw Conclusion	Item 4 Explain Conclusion	Item 5 Evaluate Design
			Presentation	Data Quality			
		2 Points	2 Points	3 Points	2 Points	2 Points	2 Points
Singapore	68 (2.7)	53 (5.0)	91 (1.8)	81 (2.1)	93 (2.2)	42 (4.0)	46 (5.4)
Czech Republic	59 (2.3)	60 (3.6)	71 (2.8)	63 (3.0)	86 (3.1)	28 (3.4)	48 (4.5)
†† Switzerland	57 (1.9)	55 (4.8)	79 (2.7)	79 (2.9)	85 (3.0)	11 (1.5)	36 (5.2)
† Scotland	51 (2.3)	44 (3.8)	72 (3.9)	70 (3.3)	81 (3.7)	18 (2.4)	23 (3.9)
Iran, Islamic Rep.	50 (3.5)	52 (4.3)	52 (6.7)	47 (5.5)	86 (4.5)	36 (7.7)	26 (3.2)
Sweden	50 (2.2)	51 (3.9)	55 (3.3)	65 (3.0)	77 (2.9)	18 (2.5)	34 (4.7)
Canada	48 (2.1)	39 (4.0)	64 (3.1)	59 (2.6)	76 (1.9)	26 (2.4)	27 (4.1)
New Zealand	48 (2.1)	46 (3.2)	61 (3.4)	54 (2.0)	70 (2.5)	33 (2.8)	25 (3.5)
Norway	42 (1.8)	43 (2.4)	55 (3.1)	57 (3.8)	68 (4.5)	6 (1.3)	21 (3.4)
Spain	41 (2.3)	44 (4.2)	51 (3.9)	43 (3.2)	74 (3.3)	17 (2.2)	19 (3.2)
Portugal	36 (2.4)	27 (3.9)	39 (3.9)	36 (2.9)	74 (4.3)	25 (2.8)	13 (3.2)
Cyprus	29 (2.9)	14 (3.1)	42 (4.9)	44 (4.6)	47 (5.1)	18 (3.0)	10 (2.8)
Countries Not Satisfying Guidelines for Sample Participation Rates (See Appendix A for Details):							
Australia	59 (2.2)	55 (4.7)	79 (3.4)	79 (2.3)	89 (2.6)	23 (3.5)	30 (3.6)
² England	68 (2.1)	66 (3.8)	82 (2.5)	75 (1.6)	89 (2.6)	36 (4.5)	59 (4.1)
Netherlands	43 (2.7)	45 (2.7)	46 (5.2)	52 (4.2)	77 (5.0)	12 (2.6)	23 (3.0)
United States	48 (2.2)	33 (2.6)	64 (3.7)	59 (3.2)	82 (3.1)	27 (3.3)	24 (2.6)
Countries Not Meeting Age/Grade Specifications (See Appendix A for Details):							
Colombia	26 (2.3)	14 (3.7)	43 (5.2)	43 (4.4)	41 (4.8)	8 (1.6)	6 (1.6)
³ Romania	63 (2.6)	63 (4.9)	59 (3.7)	68 (5.6)	82 (3.2)	30 (4.2)	73 (4.9)
Slovenia	49 (2.0)	37 (4.0)	75 (2.9)	57 (2.8)	81 (2.8)	12 (2.8)	34 (3.6)
International Average	49 (0.5)	44 (0.9)	62 (0.9)	59 (0.8)	77 (0.8)	22 (0.8)	30 (0.9)

SOURCE: IEA Third International Mathematics and Science Study (TIMSS), 1994-95.

* Eighth grade in most countries; see Table 2 for information about the grades tested in each country.

• Percent of total possible points on each item averaged over students.

▼ Average of percentage scores across items; all items weighted equally.

† Met guidelines for sample participation rates only after replacement schools were included (see Appendix A for details)

1 National Desired Population does not cover all of International Desired Population (see Table A.2) - German-speaking cantons only.

2 National Defined Population covers less than 90 percent of National Desired Population for the main assessment (see Table A.2).

3 School-level exclusions for performance assessment exceed 25% of the National Desired Population (see Table A.2).

() Standard errors appear in parentheses. Because results are rounded to the nearest whole number, some totals may appear inconsistent.

In the Containers task, students were given three containers of different insulating capacity, for example, metal, ceramic, and plastic, and were asked to find out which one would keep a hot drink warm for the longest time. They also received thermometers, a clock, a piece of card to use as a fan, and a supply of hot water. The students were instructed to pour a measure of hot water into each of the containers, and to take the temperature in each one over a ten-minute interval. They were provided with a pre-designed data table in which to record their observations. This task assessed students' ability to make and record measurements of temperature and probed their understanding of the concept of insulation. Figure 1.9 presents the task with sample student responses and scoring criteria for a fully-correct response. This task was administered to fourth-grade students only.

In general, this was a difficult task for fourth graders. Although most students in most countries were able to use a laboratory thermometer, in many cases, the data gathered were incomplete or contained small inaccuracies in measurement (Table 1.10, Item 1 – average percentage scores: 91% and 56%). Students did reasonably well in identifying the container that kept water hottest (Item 2 – average percentage score: 48%), but almost none could explain insulating capacity in terms of the materials from which the containers were made.

An interesting misconception appeared when students were asked to apply their findings to a different situation – that of keeping ice cream cold. While 15% of students internationally (Item 4) recognized that the container that was best for keeping a hot drink warm would also be best for keeping ice cream cold, almost none could explain why (Item 5). About one-quarter of the students seemed to see the ice cream as an opposite case, explaining that the container in which the temperature of a hot drink declined most rapidly would be the one to keep ice cream cold the longest.

CONTAINERS

FIGURE 1.9 - CONTAINERS FULL-TASK EXAMPLE AND SCORING CRITERIA – FOURTH GRADE

INTRODUCTION TO TASK

CONTAINERS

At this station you should have:

Three containers (or cups) marked A, B, C
Three thermometers
A clock or watch
A container with very hot water. BE CAREFUL NOT TO SPILL HOT WATER.
Pieces of card to use as a fan if you wish
A roll of paper to wipe up spills
A measuring cup

Read <u>ALL</u> directions carefully.

Your task:

Find out which of the containers will keep a hot drink warm for the longest time.

This is what you should do:

- Place a thermometer in each of the containers <u>BEFORE</u> the hot water is poured in. Your teacher will pour the hot water when you are ready. BE CAREFUL. THE WATER IS <u>VERY HOT</u>.

- Measure the temperature on each thermometer as soon as the hot water is poured in.
- Write these measurements and the time in the table on the opposite page.

- Now you will take measurements over a total of 10 minutes.
    → Decide how often to read each thermometer.
    → Write your measurements in the table on the opposite page.

page 1   TASK S6-P1

ITEMS 1, 2, AND 3

1. Table of Measurements:

Time	Temperature of Container A	Temperature of Container B	Temperature of Container C
2:28	0	0	0
2:32	50	60	50
2:35	50	60	50
2:36	50	60	50
2:38	50	60	40
2:39	50	50½	40

2. Look at the table. Which container keeps a hot drink warm for the longest time?

cupB
plastic

3. Why do you think this container was best for keeping a hot drink warm?

Because it
holds the heat

Please turn the page.

TASK S6-P1   page 2

48

ITEMS 4 AND 5

4. Which container do you think would be the best for keeping ice-cream cold?

plastic

5. Why do you think this container will keep ice-cream cold the longest?

Becase it will keep out the heat

**WIPE UP ANY SPILLS AND POUR THE WATER OUT.
LEAVE THE STATION AS YOU FOUND IT.**

page 3   TASK S6-P1

CRITERIA FOR FULLY-CORRECT RESPONSE

Item 1 - Measure temperatures and record data in table. Student is scored both on proper use of the thermometer and on the quality of data gathering.

Ability to use thermometer. Does not require assistance in proper use of the thermometer (Based on adminstrator notes on any special assitance provided.)
Total Possible Points: 1

Quality of data gathering. i) Records times and temperatures for 5 or more temperature points per container. ii) Times cover full 10-minute range. iii) Trend in the temperature is reasonable: temperature declines with time in one or more of the cups. (One cup may be too well insulated to give measurable declines in 10 minutes.)
Total Possible Points: 3

Item 2 - Identify container that keeps hot drink warm longest.
i) Identifies correct container (based on administrator notes). ii) Container identified is consistent with the data in table.
Total Possible Points: 2

Item 3 - Explain why container retains heat. i) Relates material of containers to their ability to retain or transfer heat. ii) Includes comparison of different containers based on heat transfer.
iii) Logically applies any additional relevant information (stirring, thickness of container, size differences, etc.).
Total Possible Points: 2

Item 4 - Predict best container for keeping ice cream cold. Identifies the same container that best keeps hot drink warm.
Total Possible Points: 1

Item 5 - Explain why container keeps ice cream cold. i) Relates material of containers to their ability to retain or transfer heat.
ii) Includes comparison of different containers based on heat transfer.
iii) Logically applies any additional relevant information provided (stirring, thickness of container, size difference, etc.).
Total Possible Points: 2

Table 1.10 Containers Task: Average Percentage Score on Items – Fourth Grade*

Country	Overall Task Average▼	Average Percentage Scores on Items●					
		Item 1 Measure Temperatures and Record in Table		Item 2 Identify Best Insulator	Item 3 Explain Best Insulator	Item 4 Apply to Ice Cream	Item 5 Explain Application
		Ability to Use Thermometer	Quality of Data Gathering				
		1 Points	3 Points	2 Points	2 Points	1 Point	2 Points
Cyprus	42 (1.3)**	- -	82 (3.8)	60 (4.5)	6 (1.5)	4 (1.9)	1 (0.6)
Canada	40 (1.1)	94 (2.1)	69 (2.8)	56 (2.7)	7 (1.1)	14 (2.4)	3 (0.8)
†† New Zealand	33 (1.4)	95 (1.8)	38 (3.3)	50 (4.4)	3 (0.8)	10 (1.9)	1 (0.6)
Iran, Islamic Rep.	30 (3.5)	63 (7.6)	49 (5.3)	39 (5.3)	9 (1.8)	17 (4.2)	2 (1.4)
Portugal	26 (1.9)	78 (5.5)	31 (4.7)	33 (5.0)	3 (1:3)	11 (2.3)	2 (1.0)
Countries Not Satisfying Guidelines for Sample Participation Rates (See Appendix A for Details):							
Australia	39 (0.8)	93 (2.8)	57 (3.9)	65 (2.5)	5 (1.4)	14 (2.7)	3 (0.9)
Hong Kong	41 (1.3)	99 (0.6)	58 (2.9)	56 (3.8)	11 (2.8)	18 (3.0)	5 (1.2)
United States	40 (1.1)	98 (0.7)	64 (3.1)	32 (3.5)	8 (1.2)	31 (3.5)	4 (1.0)
Countries Not Meeting Age/Grade Specifications (See Appendix A for Details):							
Slovenia	38 (1.3)	100 (0.0)	54 (4.0)	45 (3.2)	4 (1.5)	18 (3.1)	7 (1.5)
International Average	37 (0.6)	91 (1.1)	56 (1.3)	48 (1.3)	6 (0.5)	15 (1.0)	3 (0.3)

SOURCE: IEA Third International Mathematics and Science Study (TIMSS), 1994-95.

* Fourth grade in most countries; see Table 2 for information about the grades tested in each country.
● Percent of total possible points on each item averaged over students.
▼ Average of percentage scores across items; all items weighted equally.
A dash (-) indicates data are not available. Ability to use thermometer was not recorded in Cyprus.
**Overall task average includes an estimated average percentage score of 97% for the missing item based on overall relative country performance and international item difficulty.
† Met guidelines for sample participation rates only after replacement schools were included (see Appendix A for details)
†† School-level exclusions for performance assessment exceed 25% of the National Desired Population (see Table A.3).
() Standard errors appear in parentheses. Because results are rounded to the nearest whole number, some totals may appear inconsistent.

The Shadows task measures both science and mathematics concepts and skills and is one of the two "combination" tasks. Students were asked to move an object (a square card on a stand) placed between a light source and a screen to investigate how the positions of the light source, the card, and the screen are related to the size of the shadow cast upon the screen. At the eighth grade, Items 1 and 2 (Figure 1.10) were intended to assess students' ability to follow directions, report on their observations, and use their conceptual knowledge of light and shadow to explain why the shadow was always larger than the card. Item 3 asked students to find and record at least three positions of the light and the card that would make the shadow twice the size of the card. Students then were asked to conduct an investigation to find a general rule for varying the distance between the light and the card and the card and the screen so that the shadow is always twice the size of the card. In Item 4, students were asked to describe their investigation. They were required to present their measurements in tabular form (Item 5) and then to derive the general rule (Item 6).

To do well on this task, it was important to understand how shadows are formed and that light travels in straight lines. In addition, the ability to recognize similar triangles and apply some of their properties could be very helpful in deriving a mathematical rule. However, it was also possible to arrive at a generalization empirically, without considering (or at least without explicitly referring to) similar triangles formed by the light rays, the card, and the screen.

The fourth-grade version of the Shadows task (Figure 1.11) provided simpler, more explicit directions and a table for recording the data, and placed the explanation item much later in the task, after students had more experience with the phenomenon. For fourth-grade students, except for the last two items, Shadows was largely a procedural task based on following directions. Thus, no performance comparisons are possible between the two grades, even for items that appear identical.

Except for the initial observation item (Table 1.11, Item 1 – average percentage score: 75%), this task proved difficult for most eighth-grade students. In conducting the investigations, students in some countries either assumed that they need not present new measurements or failed to list data in organized tabular form. Many estimated distances "by eye" rather than by measuring. Most students achieving full credit on deducing a general rule (Item 6 – average percentage score: 21%) based their answers on empirical data rather than a geometric approach. However, in a few instances careful investigations were carried out, with measurements so precisely done that students could actually deduce the mathematical "rule" from their empirical data. About 2% of students internationally were successful at using a mathematical approach based on recognition of similar triangles to "find a rule when the shadow will always be twice the size of the card."

Even though it was structured differently, the fourth-grade students also had a lot of difficulty with this task (Table 1.12). The first four items were procedural and were guided by explicit directions. To begin, students had only to observe and describe in general what happened when they moved the light nearer to and further from the card (Items 1 and 2), which they managed quite well. Then students were asked to measure the width of the shadow and the distance from light to card (Items 3 and 4), which they found much more problematic. In the last three items, students were asked to find and record three positions where the shadow was twice as wide as the card, explain why the shadow is always larger than the card, and find a rule that tells when the shadow will always be twice as wide as the card. These tasks were clearly beyond the grasp of the fourth-grade students.

SHADOWS

51

FIGURE 1.10 - SHADOWS FULL-TASK EXAMPLE AND SCORING CRITERIA – EIGHTH GRADE

ITEMS 1 AND 2

SHADOWS

At this station you should have:

Flashlight (or torch) on a stand (this will be called "the light")
5 cm sq. card on a stand
Screen on which to form a shadow of the card
Meter ruler
30 cm ruler

Read ALL directions carefully.

When the card is between the light and the screen, the card makes a shadow on the screen.

Your task:

Find out how the size of the shadow changes as you move the card.

This is what you should do:

- Keep the card still and move the light closer to the card and further away.

1. What happens to the size of the shadow?

   When you move the light closer to the card the shadow gets bigger and when you move the light away the shadow gets smaller.

2. Why is the shadow always larger than the card? You may draw a picture or diagram as <u>part</u> of your answer.

   The shadow is always larger than the card because as the lights rays travel they get wider. When they hit the card they are narrower than when they hit the wall. The shadow is the light which gets blocked out by the card.

   This means the light get reflected off the card on an outward angle which makes the shadow bigger

TASK SM1-P2

ITEMS 3 AND 4

3. Now find at least three positions where you can put the light and the card to make a shadow twice as wide as the card. Record the distance from the card to the screen and from the light to the card for these three positions.

   1) *13.5 cm from card to screen   13.5 cm from card to light.*
   2) *15 cm from card to screen   15.5 cm from card to light*
   3) *10 cm from card to screen   9.5 cm from card to light*

   You are now going to do an investigation to try to find a general rule for how far away from the screen the card and the light should be placed to make the shadow twice as wide as the card.

   You will need to:

   - decide what to measure
   - decide how to present your measurements clearly and simply
   - draw what conclusions you can from your measurements

4. Describe what you did in your investigation. A picture may be useful.

   For my investigation I put a ruler at the back of a box. I then moved the light around until the shadow was twice as big as the card. I then measured the distances from the card to screen and from the card to the light. I repeated this 3 time using the lights in different positions.

   Please turn the page.

ITEMS 5 AND 6

5. Present your measurements in as clear a way as possible.

Position number	distance from screen to card	distance from card to light (cm)
1	13.5 cm	13.5 cm
2	15 cm	15.5 cm
3	10 cm	9.5 cm

6. What general conclusion can you draw from these results? Try to write a rule that describes when the shadow will always be twice as wide as the card.

From these results I draw the conclusion that the card must be as far away (approximately) from the screen as it from the light.

Rule — To find a shadow twice the size of a card place the card half way between the screen and the light.

PUT THE MATERIALS BACK THE WAY YOU FOUND THEM SO THAT SOMEONE ELSE CAN USE THIS STATION

page 3   TASK SM1-P2

CRITERIA FOR FULLY-CORRECT RESPONSE

Item 1 - Describe how shadow size changes in response to distance of light. i) Comments appropriately on the size of shadow. ii) Comments on the relationship between the distance from light and size of shadow. *Total Possible Points: 2*

Item 2 - Explain why shadow is larger than card. i) Includes concept of light traveling in a straight line and spreading out from a source. ii) Explanation or diagram shows how the shadow is formed. *Total Possible Points: 2*

Item 3 - Record distances for three positions where shadow is twice as large as card. i) Records at least 3 measurements where shadow is twice the size of card. ii) Measurements are paired: distance from light to card and distance from card to screen. iii) Measurements are plausible: the distance from card to screen and distance from light to card are equal (within ±10%). *Total Possible Points: 2*

Item 4 - Describe investigation. i) Includes description of how measurements were taken. ii) Includes taking measurements of both distances and shadow width. *Total Possible Points: 2*

Item 5 - Present measurements. i) Measurements presented in a list, table or by graph. ii) Measurements are clearly and completely understandable with appropriate units, labels, and descriptors. *Total Possible Points: 2*

Item 6 - Write a general rule to describe when shadow will always be twice as wide as card. i) Summarizes data in sentences, formula, or diagram. ii) Indicates that shadow will be twice as wide as card when the distance from light to screen is twice the distance from light to card. *Total Possible Points: 2*

FIGURE 1.11 - SHADOWS | ITEMS AND SCORING CRITERIA – FOURTH GRADE

SHADOWS

At this station you should have:

Flashlight (or torch) on a stand (this will be called "the light.")
A 5 cm sq. card on a stand
Screen on which to form a shadow of the card
Meter ruler
30 cm ruler

Read ALL directions carefully.

When the card is between the light and the screen, the card makes a shadow on the screen.

Your task:

Find out how the size of the shadow changes as you move the card and the light.

This is what you should do:

- Keep the card in one place and move the light closer to the card.

1. What happens to the size of the shadow when you move the light closer to the card?

- Keep the card in one place and move the light further away from the card.

2. What happens to the size of the shadow when you move the light further from the card?

3. Put the card 5 cm from the screen. Put the light 10 cm behind the card. How wide is the shadow?

4. Put the card 10 cm from the screen and move the light until the shadow is twice as wide as the card. Measure the distance from the light to the card. Write your measurement in the table below.

5. Find three more places to put the light and the card where the shadow is twice as wide as the card. For each place, make the same measurements as you made before and write them in the table. Be sure to include the units for each measurement.

Distance from card to screen	Distance from light to card
10 cm	

6. Why is the shadow always larger than the card? You may draw a picture as <u>part</u> of your answer.

7. Find a rule that tells when the shadow will ALWAYS be twice as wide as the card.

Task layout condensed for display

Figure 1.11 (cont.) Shadows – Fourth Grade

Criteria for Fully-Correct Response

Item 1 - Describe how shadow size changes when card is moved closer to light. i) States that shadow becomes larger as card is brought closer to light.
Total Possible Points: 1

Item 2 - Describe how shadow size changes when card is moved further from light. i) States that shadow becomes smaller as card is pulled further from light.
Total Possible Points: 1

Item 3 - Measure width of shadow when card and light are placed at specific distances. Determines width by *measurement*. Measurement is accurate (7.5 cm ± 8 mm) for card 5 cm from screen and light 10 cm from card.
Total Possible Points: 1

Item 4 - Measure distance from light to card where shadow is twice the size of card. i) Distance from light to card is equal to the distance from card to screen (or half the distance from light to screen). ii) With card 10 cm from screen, correct measurement is 10 cm ± 5 mm.
Total Possible Points: 2

Item 5 - Record distances for three more positions where shadow is twice as large as card. i) Table is complete. ii) Measurements are plausible: the distance from light to card is equal to distance from card to screen, within ± 10%.
Total Possible Points: 2

Item 6 - Explain why shadow is always larger than card.
i) Includes concept of light traveling in a straight line and spreading out from a source. ii) Explanation or diagram shows how shadow is formed.
Total Possible Points: 2

Item 7 - Find a rule to predict when shadow will be twice as wide as card. i) States that shadow will always be twice as wide as card when the distance from light to screen is twice the distance from light to card.
Total Possible Points: 2

Table 1.11 Shadows Task: Average Percentage Score on Items – Eighth Grade*

Country	Overall Task Average▼	Average Percentage Scores on Items●					
		Item 1 Describe Observation 2 Points	Item 2 Explain Observation 2 Points	Item 3 Problem Solve and Record Distances 2 Points	Item 4 Describe Investigation 2 Points	Item 5 Present Measurements 2 Points	Item 6 Conclude and Generalize 2 Points
Singapore	50 (3.5)	90 (1.8)	55 (6.0)	41 (4.8)	39 (3.5)	46 (6.0)	29 (4.6)
Sweden	45 (1.9)	82 (2.4)	43 (3.9)	57 (3.9)	30 (3.3)	27 (4.0)	32 (3.5)
Iran, Islamic Rep.	43 (1.5)	84 (2.8)	57 (3.9)	33 (4.1)	23 (2.4)	24 (2.6)	37 (2.8)
†† Switzerland	41 (2.1)	80 (3.5)	44 (4.9)	43 (3.6)	29 (3.7)	22 (3.2)	32 (3.3)
Norway	39 (2.0)	75 (3.0)	28 (3.1)	51 (3.4)	25 (2.5)	18 (3.1)	35 (4.3)
Czech Republic	37 (1.9)	87 (2.7)	48 (2.9)	32 (3.5)	27 (2.9)	8 (2.4)	19 (3.8)
† Scotland	36 (2.4)	83 (3.3)	24 (3.3)	31 (4.0)	28 (4.3)	36 (3.5)	16 (3.4)
Spain	36 (1.7)	78 (2.9)	40 (3.8)	29 (2.7)	37 (3.7)	16 (3.0)	16 (2.1)
Canada	35 (1.6)	75 (2.6)	21 (3.2)	34 (2.8)	30 (2.3)	28 (3.8)	19 (2.5)
New Zealand	29 (2.0)	70 (3.5)	17 (2.1)	15 (1.7)	21 (2.7)	35 (2.8)	13 (2.5)
Portugal	25 (1.5)	65 (3.2)	27 (3.7)	24 (2.7)	16 (2.6)	11 (2.3)	7 (2.1)
Cyprus	18 (1.5)	64 (4.8)	14 (3.2)	8 (2.2)	12 (2.7)	3 (1.4)	9 (2.3)
Countries Not Satisfying Guidelines for Sample Participation Rates (See Appendix A for Details):							
Australia	36 (1.9)	67 (3.7)	24 (3.4)	39 (3.8)	32 (4.1)	28 (4.4)	25 (4.6)
² England	46 (2.3)	77 (2.9)	33 (3.9)	23 (3.3)	47 (3.2)	71 (3.7)	23 (3.0)
Netherlands	35 (2.8)	55 (4.1)	50 (5.2)	33 (3.7)	27 (3.3)	25 (4.3)	23 (3.9)
United States	28 (1.9)	64 (4.0)	20 (2.4)	13 (2.6)	27 (2.8)	34 (3.2)	11 (2.3)
Countries Not Meeting Age/Grade Specifications (See Appendix A for Details):							
Colombia	22 (2.5)	54 (5.4)	22 (2.7)	21 (4.1)	17 (3.5)	14 (4.9)	5 (1.9)
³ Romania	36 (2.8)	92 (2.3)	28 (3.6)	24 (4.8)	26 (4.8)	17 (3.1)	26 (5.1)
Slovenia	31 (1.8)	76 (3.3)	29 (3.0)	24 (2.7)	24 (2.9)	12 (2.1)	19 (3.6)
International Average	35 (0.5)	75 (0.8)	33 (0.8)	30 (0.8)	27 (0.8)	25 (0.8)	21 (0.8)

SOURCE: IEA Third International Mathematics and Science Study (TIMSS), 1994-95.

* Eighth grade in most countries; see Table 2 for information about the grades tested in each country.

● Percent of total possible points on each item averaged over students.

▼ Average of percentage scores across items; all items weighted equally.

† Met guidelines for sample participation rates only after replacement schools were included (see Appendix A for details)

1 National Desired Population does not cover all of International Desired Population (see Table A.2) - German-speaking cantons only.

2 National Defined Population covers less than 90 percent of National Desired Population for the main assessment (see Table A.2).

3 School-level exclusions for performance assessment exceed 25% of the National Desired Population (see Table A.2).

() Standard errors appear in parentheses. Because results are rounded to the nearest whole number, some totals may appear inconsistent.

Shadows Task: Average Percentage Score on Items – Fourth Grade* Table 1.12

Country	Overall Task Average▼	Average Percentage Scores on Items●						
		Item 1 Describe Shadow: Closer 1 Point	Item 2 Describe Shadow: Further 1 Point	Item 3 Measure Shadow Width 1 Point	Item 4 Measure Distance 2 Points	Item 5 Record 3 More Measurements 2 Points	Item 6 Explain Shadow Size 2 Points	Item 7 Find General Rule 2 Points
Canada	36 (1.7)	72 (3.0)	70 (3.1)	36 (2.9)	22 (2.4)	29 (2.3)	12 (1.8)	8 (1.2)
ᵗᵗ New Zealand	34 (1.0)	86 (2.7)	82 (2.9)	32 (3.3)	16 (2.7)	14 (2.4)	5 (1.4)	3 (1.0)
Portugal	27 (1.6)	66 (4.8)	63 (4.9)	25 (4.1)	16 (3.3)	12 (1.8)	4 (1.3)	0 (0.0)
Iran, Islamic Rep.	26 (2.1)	61 (5.9)	63 (5.8)	13 (3.0)	18 (4.2)	15 (2.7)	7 (2.4)	3 (1.2)
Cyprus	16 (1.6)	47 (4.7)	39 (4.7)	11 (2.8)	7 (2.1)	5 (1.8)	3 (1.8)	1 (0.4)
Countries Not Satisfying Guidelines for Sample Participation Rates (See Appendix A for Details):								
Australia	33 (1.6)	71 (4.5)	72 (2.3)	31 (6.0)	20 (2.8)	27 (2.7)	4 (1.3)	6 (1.9)
Hong Kong	30 (1.6)	65 (5.0)	62 (3.3)	24 (4.3)	17 (3.1)	17 (3.1)	17 (5.0)	5 (2.0)
United States	33 (1.2)	79 (2.6)	81 (2.9)	33 (3.7)	19 (2.7)	8 (1.5)	7 (1.6)	3 (1.3)
Countries Not Meeting Age/Grade Specifications (See Appendix A for Details):								
Slovenia	32 (1.8)	77 (4.8)	73 (4.9)	32 (3.5)	23 (4.0)	12 (2.5)	4 (1.1)	6 (2.1)
International Average	30 (0.5)	69 (1.4)	67 (1.3)	26 (1.3)	18 (1.0)	15 (0.8)	7 (0.8)	4 (0.5)

SOURCE: IEA Third International Mathematics and Science Study (TIMSS), 1994-95.

* Fourth grade in most countries; see Table 2 for information about the grades tested in each country.
● Percent of total possible points on each item averaged over students.
▼ Average of percentage scores across items; all items weighted equally.
† Met guidelines for sample participation rates only after replacement schools were included (see Appendix A for details)
¹ School-level exclusions for performance assessment exceed 25% of the National Desired Population (see Table A.3).
() Standard errors appear in parentheses. Because results are rounded to the nearest whole number, some totals may appear inconsistent.

The Plasticine task also combines mathematics and science concepts and skills and is thus a "combination" task. Students were provided with a simple equal-arm balance and a supply of plasticine (modeling clay) and asked to use the balance to make lumps of plasticine of different weights. Eighth-grade students were given 20g and 50g weights and asked to form four lumps of plasticine: 20g, 10g, 15g, and 35g in weight (in that order), and to explain their strategy for forming each one. This task was intended to measure student understanding of the principle of the balance and the ability to use it, as well as mathematical problem solving in non-routine situations. Although the first item is a simple matter of building up a lump of plasticine that balances the 20g weight, the other three lumps can be made only by combining and dividing lumps in various combinations. These three problems require carefully thought-out problem-solving strategies but are essentially the same task, although of increasing complexity. Figure 1.13 presents the task, with a sample response and scoring criteria for a fully-correct response. All lumps of plasticine were handed in at the end of the session and the weights verified by the administrator.

The task for fourth-grade students was basically the same, except that the fourth graders were given only one 20g weight with the balance, and the required lumps were 20g, 10g, 30g, 15g. Items 1A, 1B and 2A, 2B are the same for both grade levels, and Items 4A, 4B for fourth-grade students correspond to Items 3A, 3B for eighth-grade students. Figure 1.14 shows the task for fourth graders.

In order to keep administration costs to a minimum, countries were encouraged to use balances constructed from everyday materials according to a design provided by the TIMSS International Study Center. Although these balances worked quite well, students at both grade levels had difficulty achieving accurate results. To compensate for this lack of precision, the scoring rubrics allowed a tolerance of ±10% for the two larger lumps and ±20% for the two smaller ones. However, some 30% of the eighth-grade students did not achieve this level of accuracy.

Eighth-grade students had no difficulty with the straightforward task of making a 20g lump (Table 1.13, Item 1A – average percentage score: 93%), or in describing how they accomplished this (Item 1B – average percentage score: 86%). The most difficult to make proved to be the 15g lump (Item 3B – average percentage score: 37%). The most popular strategy was to make a 20g lump; halve it, using the balance to obtain a 10g lump; and halve that to obtain a 5g lump that was then added to the 10g lump. The most popular strategy for Item 4B (making a 35g lump), was to use the weights and previously made lumps to build up a new lump of 35g: e.g., "I put the 50g weight on one side and my 15g lump on the other and added to the 15g side until they balanced."

Some of the eighth-grade students showed a lack of comprehension of how an equal-arm balance operates, and either attempted to use the slope of the balance arm to estimate weights, or (where commercially produced balances were used) used the small mechanism intended for balancing the instrument before use (zeroing) and tried to calibrate it (mentally) to determine weight: e.g., "I put the 20g weight in the scale and added plasticine till it reached this mark." Here the student has drawn the zeroing bar, arbitrarily named the zero point in the center as 20g, and "estimated" a marker about 4 divisions to the left to be 35g. The verified weight was 24 grams.

Fourth-grade students also found the task of making a 20g lump fairly easy (Table 1.14, Item 1A – average percentage score: 80%), but describing how they did it was more challenging (Item 1B – average percentage score: 52%). The other tasks, all of which involved the use of the balance to divide and sometimes combine previously made lumps, were very difficult for these students.

PLASTICINE

FIGURE 1.12 - PLASTICINE   FULL-TASK EXAMPLE AND SCORING CRITERIA — EIGHTH GRADE

ITEM 1

PLASTICINE

At this station you should have:

    Some plasticine
    A balance
    Plastic bags
    A 20 g and a 50 g mass (weight)
    Colored small circular sticky labels

Read ALL directions carefully.

> **Your task:**
>
> Use the balance to weigh different amounts of plasticine as carefully as you can. Then explain how you made them.

    Before starting the task:

        MAKE SURE THE PANS ARE BALANCED WHEN EMPTY.

        IF THEY ARE NOT, PUT YOUR HAND UP AND TELL THE TEACHER.

1a. Use the balance to make a lump of plasticine that weighs 20 g.

    • When you have made the 20 g lump, write 20 g on a colored label and stick it on the lump. Put the lump in a plastic bag.

1b. Write down how you made the 20 g lump.

I put the 20g weight in one of the treys on the balance. I then started putting small amounts of plastic on the other trey. gradually the balance evenened out untill it was the same on both sides. I knew the plasticine weighed 20g.

TASK SM2-P2

ITEMS 2 AND 3

2a. Use the balance to make a lump of plasticine that weighs 10 g.

    • When you have made the 10 g lump, write 10 g on a colored label and stick it on the lump. Put the lump in the plastic bag with the 20 g lump.

2b. Write down how you made the 10 g lump.

I made another 20g lump using the same method as before. Then I broke it in half and placed one on each trey on the balance. If one was heavier than the other I would break some of it off and put it on the lighter one. Eventually both lumps weighed the same and I knew each one would weigh 10grams.

3a. Use the balance to make a lump of plasticine that weighs 15 g.

    • When you have made the 15 g lump, write 15 g on a colored label and stick it on the lump. Place the 15 g lump in the plastic bag together with the other lumps.

3b. Write down how you made the 15 g lump.

I used the 20g weight and the 10g lump, and I placed each one on a trey. I then made a lump that weighed the same. I then split it in half, I took the weights off the trey and using the same method as above, I made them even, so each would weigh 15 grams

Please turn the page.

TASK SM2-P2

ITEM 4 AND ADMINISTRATOR'S MEASUREMENTS

4a. Use the balance to make a lump of plasticine that weighs 35 g.

- When you have made the 35 g lump, write 35 g on a colored label and stick it on the lump. Place the 35 g lump in the plastic bag with the other lumps.

4b. Write down how you made the 35 g lump.

I put the 20g ~~lump~~ weight on a trey with the 15 g lump I just made. I kept putting plasticine on the other empty trey until they were even, so the lump would weigh 35g

ADMINISTRATOR'S MEASUREMENTS

	4a	1a	3a	2a
Expected	35	20	15	10
Actual	35	19	15	10

HAND IN THE BAG WITH THE LUMPS OF PLASTICINE YOU HAVE WEIGHED. MAKE SURE YOUR NAME IS ON THE BAG

LEAVE EVERYTHING ELSE AS YOU FOUND IT.

page 3   TASK SM2-P2

CRITERIA FOR FULLY-CORRECT RESPONSE

Item 1a - Weigh a 20 g lump of plasticine. Lump has correct mass (20 ± 2 g). (Based on administrator measurement.)
Total Possible Points: 1

Item 1b - Describe strategy for making 20 g lump of plasticine.
i) Method includes use of balance. ii) Method plausible for obtaining desired mass.
Total Possible Points: 2

Item 2a - Weigh a 10 g lump of plasticine. Lump has correct mass (10 ± 2 g). (Based on administrator measurement.)
Total Possible Points: 2

Item 2b - Describe strategy for making 10 g lump of plasticine.
i) Method includes use of balance. ii) Method plausible for obtaining desired mass.
Total Possible Points: 2

Item 3a - Weigh a 15 g lump of plasticine. Lump has correct mass (15 ± 3 g). (Based on administrator measurement.)
Total Possible Points: 1

Item 3b - Describe strategy for making 15 g lump of plasticine.
i) Method includes use of balance. ii) Method plausible for obtaining desired mass.
Total Possible Points: 2

Item 4a - Weigh a 35 g lump of plasticine. Lump has correct mass (35 ± 3 g). (Based on administrator measurement.)
Total Possible Points: 2

Item 4b - Describe strategy for making 35 g lump of plasticine.
i) Method includes use of balance. ii) Method plausible for obtaining desired mass.
Total Possible Points:2

FIGURE 1.13 - PLASTICINE | ITEMS AND SCORING CRITERIA – FOURTH GRADE

PLASTICINE

At this station you should have:

Some plasticine
A balance
Plastic bags
A 20 g mass (weight)
Colored small circular sticky labels

Read ALL directions carefully.

Your task:

Use the balance to weigh different amounts of plasticine as carefully as you can. Then explain how you made them.

Before starting the task:

MAKE SURE THE PANS ARE BALANCED WHEN EMPTY.

IF THEY ARE NOT, PUT YOUR HAND UP AND TELL THE TEACHER.

1a. Use the balance to make a lump of plasticine that weighs 20 g.

- When you have made the 20 g lump, write 20 g on a colored label and stick it on the lump. Put the lump in a plastic bag.

1b. Write down how you made the 20 g lump.

2a. Use the balance to make a lump of plasticine that weighs 10 g.

- When you have made the 10 g lump, write 10 g on a colored label and stick it on the lump. Put the lump in the plastic bag with the 20 g lump.

2b. Write down how you made the 10 g lump.

3a. Use the balance to make a lump of plasticine that weighs 30 g.

- When you have made the 30 g lump, write 30 g on a colored label and stick it on the lump. Place the 30 g lump in the plastic bag with the 20 g and 10 g lumps.

3b. Write down how you made theμ 30 g lump.

4a. Use the balance to make a lump of plasticine that weighs 15g.

- When you have made the 15 g lump, write 15 g on a colored label and stick it on the lump. Place the 15 g lump in the plastic bag with the other lumps.

4b. Write down how you made the 15 g lump.

CRITERIA FOR FULLY-CORRECT RESPONSE

Item 1a - Weigh a 20 g lump of plasticine. Lump has correct mass (20 ± 2 g). (Based on administrator measurement.)
Total Possible Points: 1

Item 1b - Describe strategy for making 20 g lump of plasticine.
i) Method includes use of balance. ii) Method plausible for obtaining desired mass.
Total Possible Points: 2

Item 2a - Weigh a 10 g lump of plasticine. Lump has correct mass (10 ± 2 g). (Based on administrator measurement.)
Total Possible Points: 2

Item 2b - Describe strategy for making 10 g lump of plasticine.
i) Method includes use of balance. ii) Method plausible for obtaining desired mass.
Total Possible Points: 2

Item 3a - Weigh a 30 g lump of plasticine. Lump has correct mass (30 ± 3 g). (Based on administrator measurement.)
Total Possible Points: 1

Item 3b - Describe strategy for making 30 g lump of plasticine.
i) Method includes use of balance. ii) Method plausible for obtaining desired mass.
Total Possible Points: 2

Item 4a - Weigh a 15 g lump of plasticine. Lump has correct mass (15 ± 3 g). (Based on administrator measurement.)
Total Possible Points: 2

Item 4b - Describe strategy for making 15 g lump of plasticine.
i) Method includes use of balance. ii) Method plausible for obtaining desired mass.
Total Possible Points:2

Task layout condensed for display

Table 1.13 Plasticine Task: Average Percentage Score on Items – Eighth Grade*

Country	Overall Task Average▼	Average Percentage Scores on Items●							
		Item 1A Weigh 20g Lump	Item 1B Describe Strategy 20g Lump	Item 2A Weigh 10g Lump	Item 2B Describe Strategy 10g Lump	Item 3A Weigh 15g Lump	Item 3B Describe Strategy 15g Lump	Item 4A Weigh 35g Lump	Item 4B Describe Strategy 35g Lump
		1 Points	2 Points	2 Points	2 Points	1 Points	2 Points	2 Points	2 Points
Iran, Islamic Rep.	81 (2.6)	93 (2.4)	97 (1.2)	91 (4.2)	79 (2.5)	92 (2.7)	72 (3.6)	64 (5.1)	63 (6.7)
†† Switzerland	73 (2.1)	98 (1.3)	88 (2.0)	82 (3.9)	71 (3.2)	71 (4.8)	50 (3.7)	62 (3.8)	60 (3.7)
Sweden	72 (2.9)	88 (3.5)	97 (1.0)	80 (3.5)	69 (3.1)	73 (4.3)	51 (4.6)	57 (5.4)	58 (4.4)
Czech Republic	68 (2.6)	95 (2.1)	96 (1.9)	74 (4.1)	62 (3.5)	65 (4.1)	44 (4.0)	58 (4.9)	51 (6.0)
Norway	67 (2.3)	99 (0.9)	92 (1.7)	74 (4.1)	62 (3.7)	64 (3.9)	38 (3.7)	54 (3.9)	50 (3.5)
Singapore	66 (3.3)	99 (0.7)	82 (2.7)	65 (5.2)	60 (4.9)	64 (5.6)	44 (3.9)	60 (4.7)	53 (4.0)
Canada	65 (1.9)	93 (2.0)	86 (2.1)	68 (2.9)	58 (3.1)	71 (3.6)	40 (3.9)	54 (3.4)	49 (2.9)
New Zealand	63 (2.2)	98 (0.9)	94 (1.7)	56 (3.4)	52 (3.0)	64 (2.5)	36 (3.5)	51 (3.7)	52 (3.7)
† Scotland	61 (2.5)	94 (2.6)	85 (3.0)	59 (4.1)	47 (4.1)	70 (3.3)	39 (4.0)	53 (4.5)	41 (4.2)
Cyprus	52 (2.4)	91 (3.3)	83 (3.2)	57 (3.4)	45 (3.7)	55 (4.7)	19 (4.1)	33 (5.3)	32 (4.1)
Spain	45 (2.5)	79 (4.1)	78 (3.4)	48 (4.6)	36 (4.0)	51 (4.9)	20 (3.2)	29 (4.2)	23 (3.1)
Portugal	41 (2.5)	95 (2.3)	82 (2.0)	47 (5.4)	38 (5.0)	22 (4.5)	15 (3.5)	15 (3.2)	13 (2.7)
Countries Not Satisfying Guidelines for Sample Participation Rates (See Appendix A for Details):									
Australia	73 (2.9)	97 (1.9)	94 (1.6)	73 (4.0)	69 (4.2)	71 (4.1)	60 (5.2)	57 (4.7)	64 (4.4)
² England	55 (2.4)	93 (2.5)	85 (2.1)	44 (3.7)	42 (3.6)	57 (4.8)	29 (2.8)	41 (4.9)	48 (3.3)
Netherlands	44 (2.5)	95 (1.2)	80 (3.7)	35 (4.0)	29 (3.2)	31 (4.4)	17 (2.9)	29 (4.6)	38 (4.8)
United States	53 (2.1)	91 (2.4)	65 (2.8)	50 (4.0)	34 (3.2)	76 (3.1)	24 (2.6)	46 (3.9)	40 (3.5)
Countries Not Meeting Age/Grade Specifications (See Appendix A for Details):									
Colombia	41 (2.7)	89 (3.0)	59 (3.7)	45 (5.4)	29 (4.2)	46 (4.8)	21 (4.1)	21 (4.4)	22 (4.0)
³ Romania	63 (4.1)	97 (1.7)	96 (1.7)	64 (6.1)	55 (4.8)	56 (6.4)	47 (5.6)	45 (7.1)	43 (5.8)
Slovenia	63 (1.9)	94 (1.9)	87 (3.0)	78 (3.3)	45 (4.1)	64 (4.1)	34 (3.5)	59 (3.7)	46 (4.7)
International Average	60 (0.6)	93 (0.5)	86 (0.6)	63 (1.0)	52 (0.9)	61 (1.0)	37 (0.9)	47 (1.0)	44 (1.0)

SOURCE: IEA Third International Mathematics and Science Study (TIMSS), 1994-95.

* Eighth grade in most countries; see Table 2 for information about the grades tested in each country.

● Percent of total possible points on each item averaged over students.

▼ Average of percentage scores across items; all items weighted equally.

† Met guidelines for sample participation rates only after replacement schools were included (see Appendix A for details)

1 National Desired Population does not cover all of International Desired Population (see Table A.2) - German-speaking cantons only.

2 National Defined Population covers less than 90 percent of National Desired Population for the main assessment (see Table A.2).

3 School-level exclusions for performance assessment exceed 25% of the National Desired Population (see Table A.2).

( ) Standard errors appear in parentheses. Because results are rounded to the nearest whole number, some totals may appear inconsistent.

Plasticine Task: Average Percentage Score on Items – Fourth Grade* | Table 1.14

Country	Overall Task Average▼	Average Percentage Scores on Items●							
		Item 1A Weigh 20g Lump	Item 1B Describe Strategy 20g Lump	Item 2A Weigh 10g Lump	Item 2B Describe Strategy 10g Lump	Item 3A Weigh 30g Lump	Item 3B Describe Strategy 30g Lump	Item 4A Weigh 15g Lump	Item 4B Describe Strategy 15g Lump
		1 Point	2 Points	2 Points	2 Points	1 Points	2 Points	1 Point	2 Points
Iran, Islamic Rep.	63 (3.3)	89 (2.8)	63 (4.9)	80 (3.1)	50 (5.5)	64 (4.1)	47 (6.3)	69 (4.5)	39 (4.7)
Canada	43 (1.7)	83 (2.6)	62 (3.6)	37 (3.0)	28 (2.2)	37 (3.9)	28 (2.7)	52 (4.4)	20 (2.0)
†† New Zealand	35 (2.0)	78 (3.7)	62 (3.9)	24 (2.8)	20 (2.5)	29 (3.5)	25 (2.9)	28 (4.1)	10 (1.9)
Cyprus	30 (2.1)	76 (5.5)	40 (3.1)	31 (4.4)	14 (2.4)	26 (6.7)	16 (3.7)	30 (5.1)	6 (1.9)
Portugal	24 (2.3)	87 (3.6)	46 (4.3)	25 (5.2)	12 (3.4)	10 (3.3)	10 (3.3)	0 (0.0)	2 (1.3)
Countries Not Satisfying Guidelines for Sample Participation Rates (See Appendix A for Details):									
Australia	40 (2.1)	83 (4.4)	60 (3.9)	42 (3.9)	24 (3.1)	33 (3.5)	28 (3.7)	34 (3.9)	15 (1.9)
Hong Kong	23 (1.7)	66 (3.4)	40 (4.6)	18 (4.2)	10 (2.7)	18 (3.8)	17 (3.6)	10 (2.6)	7 (2.0)
United States	31 (1.5)	75 (2.6)	36 (2.9)	30 (3.7)	13 (2.1)	26 (3.3)	14 (2.3)	47 (3.3)	7 (1.5)
Countries Not Meeting Age/Grade Specifications (See Appendix A for Details):									
Slovenia	46 (2.7)	82 (3.5)	61 (5.0)	65 (4.0)	22 (3.5)	51 (5.3)	28 (3.7)	45 (4.8)	15 (2.6)
International Average	37 (0.7)	80 (1.2)	52 (1.4)	39 (1.3)	21 (1.1)	33 (1.4)	24 (1.2)	35 (1.3)	13 (0.8)

SOURCE: IEA Third International Mathematics and Science Study (TIMSS), 1994-95.

* Fourth grade in most countries; see Table 2 for information about the grades tested in each country.

● Percent of total possible points on each item averaged over students.

▼ Average of percentage scores across items; all items weighted equally.

† Met guidelines for sample participation rates only after replacement schools were included (see Appendix A for details)

1 School-level exclusions for performance assessment exceed 25% of the National Desired Population (see Table A.3).

( ) Standard errors appear in parentheses. Because results are rounded to the nearest whole number, some totals may appear inconsistent.

In the mathematics task Dice, students were asked to explore the application of a transformation rule to a set of numbers generated by the throw of a die. Students were given a die, a shaker, and an algorithm for converting the number resulting from each throw to another number. They were asked to generate some numbers, apply the algorithm, and answer some questions about the patterns of numbers generated. Students also were provided with a table showing two examples of the transformation to be applied, and the shell of a table for recording data (the ability to construct a data table was not being assessed here). Dice is a fairly straightforward task, intended to measure students' ability to apply an arbitrary numerical algorithm, record and analyze data, and identify and explain the patterns in the data recorded. The task is identical for both populations. Scoring criteria for fully-correct responses to each item and examples of student responses are shown in Figure 1.14.

Eighth-grade students generally found the application of the algorithm easy (Table 1.15, Items 1 and 3 – average percentage score: 90%), but describing the data (Item 2 – average percentage score: 71%) and summarizing it in another table (Item 4 – average percentage score: 71%) were more difficult. Students had little difficulty extracting an item of information from the table (Item 5A – average percentage score: 83%), but providing an explanation for the pattern of data in the summary table (Item 5B – average percentage score: 33%) was much more demanding.

A similar pattern of achievement across items was found for fourth-grade students, although these students had a lower average performance level (Table 1.16 – average percentage score: 42% for fourth graders, compared with Table 1.15 average percentage score: 73% for eighth graders). The younger students also found the application of the algorithm manageable, but the less procedural questions caused them more problems. In particular, the very low scores on Item 5B reflects the difficulty noted earlier that primary-school students have in producing written explanations.

DICE

FIGURE 1.14 - DICE   FULL-TASK EXAMPLE AND SCORING CRITERIA – EIGHTH AND FOURTH GRADES

ITEM 1

DICE

At this station you should have:

One of a pair of dice (This is called a die.)
A shaker

Read ALL directions carefully.

Your task:

Find out what happens when we use a rule to change the numbers that turn up when a die is thrown.

The rule for changing the numbers is:

- If an ODD number turns up, take away 1 and record the result.
- If an EVEN number turns up, add 2 and record the result.

1. In the table below, two examples have already been recorded for you. Use the rule to find out what the other changed numbers will be. Complete the table.

Number on die	Changed numbers
1	0
2	4
3	2
4	6
5	4
6	8

It's a 3. 3 is an odd number, so I'll take away 1 and record 2.

It's a 4. 4 is an even number, so I'll add 2 and record 6.

TASK M1-P2

ITEMS 2 AND 3

2. What do you notice about the numbers you recorded?

All the numbers, once we've used the rule come out as an even number

3. Throw the die 30 times. Each time you throw the die change the numbers that turn up using the rule. Each time record the number on the die and the changed numbers. Write the numbers in the tables below.

Number on die	Changed number
5	4
6	8
5	4
3	2
1	0
4	6
3	2
4	6
2	4
2	4
4	6
5	4
4	6
1	0
6	8

Number on die	Changed number
4	6
1	0
2	4
6	8
6	8
4	6
3	2
5	4
2	4
4	6
5	4
6	8
6	8
4	6
3	2

Please turn the page.

ITEM 4 AND 5

4. Look again at the table you filled in for question number 3. How many times did you record each of the following numbers in the "Changed Number" column?

Changed Number	Number of Times Recorded
0	3
1	0
2	4
3	0
4	9
5	0
6	8
7	0
8	6

5a. What changed number did you record most? 4 (fours)

5b. Why did it happen this way?

Because twos (2) and fives (5) both get changed into a 4, when using the rule

PUT YOUR MATERIALS BACK THE WAY YOU FOUND THEM SO THAT SOMEONE ELSE CAN USE THIS STATION.

TASK M1-P2

CRITERIA FOR FULLY-CORRECT RESPONSE

Item 1 - Change numbers according to algorithm to complete table.
Applies algorithm correctly (0, 4, 2, 6, 4, 8).
Total Possible Points: 2

Item 2 - Identify and describe pattern in numbers.
i) Describes pattern that is consistent with data. ii) Patterns and trends may be one or more of the following: all numbers are even; numbers range from 0 to 8; number 4 occurs twice; rule for obtaining sequential numbers, such as +4, -2, +4, -2.
Total Possible Points: 1

Item 3 - Apply algorithm to die throws and record resulting numbers in table. i) Completes at least 25 throws of die. ii) Applies algorithm correctly.
Total Possible Points: 2

Item 4 - Count frequency of each changed number recorded in table. Response consistent with data table.
Total Possible Points: 2

Item 5a - Identify most frequently recorded number in table. Response is consistent with data.
Total Possible Points: 1

Item 5b - Explain most frequently recorded number in table. Provides plausible explanation to account for the predominance of observed number.
Total Possible Points: 1

Table 1.15 Dice Task: Average Percentage Score on Items – Eighth Grade*

Country	Overall Task Average▼	Average Percentage Scores on Items●					
		Item 1 Complete Table 2 Points	Item 2 Describe Pattern 1 Point	Item 3 Apply Algorithm 2 Points	Item 4 Count Frequencies 2 Points	Item 5A Identify Most Frequent Number 1 Point	Item 5B Explain Findings 1 Point
Singapore	84 (1.6)	97 (1.0)	90 (2.8)	95 (1.9)	84 (2.1)	95 (2.1)	44 (6.1)
†† Switzerland	79 (1.4)	91 (1.9)	86 (3.8)	94 (1.4)	69 (3.0)	86 (2.8)	45 (4.1)
Canada	77 (1.8)	92 (2.0)	84 (3.2)	90 (1.7)	75 (3.0)	88 (2.3)	31 (3.1)
† Scotland	76 (1.6)	93 (1.5)	73 (3.3)	93 (1.0)	70 (2.7)	87 (2.0)	41 (4.6)
Portugal	76 (1.8)	96 (1.3)	67 (4.5)	97 (1.2)	72 (3.2)	85 (2.9)	38 (4.9)
Sweden	74 (2.4)	94 (1.7)	65 (4.7)	92 (2.3)	71 (3.7)	81 (3.2)	44 (4.7)
Czech Republic	73 (2.5)	93 (2.1)	75 (5.2)	83 (3.1)	73 (3.3)	78 (3.7)	39 (4.7)
New Zealand	73 (1.2)	94 (1.2)	76 (2.4)	93 (1.3)	63 (2.4)	83 (2.6)	31 (3.5)
Spain	73 (2.2)	88 (2.4)	68 (3.4)	90 (2.4)	68 (3.2)	83 (3.7)	43 (5.2)
Norway	72 (1.9)	94 (2.4)	70 (4.5)	89 (2.2)	65 (3.5)	87 (2.8)	30 (4.5)
Cyprus	68 (2.2)	83 (2.6)	67 (4.3)	90 (2.4)	65 (3.2)	77 (4.8)	28 (4.7)
Iran, Islamic Rep.	58 (1.8)	83 (3.8)	34 (3.7)	78 (3.8)	72 (6.1)	73 (4.1)	9 (3.2)
Countries Not Satisfying Guidelines for Sample Participation Rates (See Appendix A for Details):							
Australia	78 (2.4)	94 (1.4)	74 (4.5)	93 (1.6)	76 (3.2)	89 (2.9)	44 (4.9)
² England	79 (1.6)	97 (1.2)	83 (2.8)	93 (1.9)	73 (2.5)	90 (3.0)	38 (3.9)
Netherlands	76 (2.2)	97 (1.1)	82 (7.1)	96 (1.6)	72 (3.3)	87 (2.9)	21 (3.7)
United States	71 (2.1)	89 (2.6)	76 (3.1)	88 (2.2)	69 (3.1)	77 (2.8)	29 (3.3)
Countries Not Meeting Age/Grade Specifications (See Appendix A for Details):							
Colombia	49 (4.0)	68 (4.2)	41 (6.8)	70 (4.9)	52 (4.5)	60 (8.4)	6 (1.8)
³ Romania	76 (2.3)	67 (6.2)	73 (4.4)	95 (2.0)	88 (3.1)	88 (3.0)	42 (5.2)
Slovenia	78 (1.4)	98 (1.1)	72 (3.9)	99 (1.0)	80 (3.0)	89 (2.8)	33 (4.3)
International Average	73 (0.5)	90 (0.6)	71 (1.0)	90 (0.5)	71 (0.8)	83 (0.8)	33 (1.0)

SOURCE: IEA Third International Mathematics and Science Study (TIMSS), 1994-95.

* Eighth grade in most countries; see Table 2 for information about the grades tested in each country.

● Percent of total possible points on each item averaged over students.

▼ Average of percentage scores across items; all items weighted equally.

† Met guidelines for sample participation rates only after replacement schools were included (see Appendix A for details)

¹ National Desired Population does not cover all of International Desired Population (see Table A.2) - German-speaking cantons only.

² National Defined Population covers less than 90 percent of National Desired Population for the main assessment (see Table A.2).

³ School-level exclusions for performance assessment exceed 25% of the National Desired Population (see Table A.2).

() Standard errors appear in parentheses. Because results are rounded to the nearest whole number, some totals may appear inconsistent.

Dice Task: Average Percentage Score on Items – Fourth Grade* | Table 1.16

Country	Overall Task Average▾	Average Percentage Scores on Items●					
		Item 1 Complete Table	Item 2 Describe Pattern	Item 3 Apply Algorithm	Item 4 Count Frequencies	Item 5A Identify Most Frequent Number	Item 5B Explain Findings
		2 Points	1 Point	2 Points	2 Points	1 Point	1 Point
Canada	46 (2.8)	77 (2.9)	41 (3.4)	63 (5.5)	40 (4.0)	48 (4.3)	5 (1.1)
†† New Zealand	39 (2.4)	67 (3.8)	31 (3.6)	65 (3.5)	27 (3.1)	42 (3.7)	5 (1.8)
Cyprus	39 (2.4)	71 (4.3)	22 (4.2)	60 (4.6)	35 (2.5)	36 (3.8)	10 (3.0)
Iran, Islamic Rep.	34 (2.9)	64 (4.9)	16 (3.8)	57 (5.0)	29 (3.8)	28 (4.6)	8 (2.9)
Portugal	28 (2.6)	72 (4.1)	21 (4.0)	41 (4.9)	14 (2.8)	16 (3.3)	4 (1.7)
Countries Not Satisfying Guidelines for Sample Participation Rates (See Appendix A for Details):							
Australia	54 (1.9)	81 (2.7)	45 (3.8)	71 (4.3)	54 (2.9)	58 (3.0)	16 (2.4)
Hong Kong	48 (3.8)	82 (3.9)	30 (4.8)	71 (6.5)	38 (5.4)	51 (4.5)	13 (2.8)
United States	45 (2.4)	71 (3.1)	43 (3.1)	68 (3.7)	31 (3.4)	47 (5.1)	7 (2.2)
Countries Not Meeting Age/Grade Specifications (See Appendix A for Details):							
Slovenia	44 (2.5)	77 (3.7)	26 (4.1)	64 (4.4)	39 (3.7)	50 (4.8)	9 (2.0)
International Average	42 (0.9)	73 (1.3)	31 (1.3)	62 (1.6)	34 (1.2)	42 (1.4)	9 (0.8)

SOURCE: IEA Third International Mathematics and Science Study (TIMSS), 1994-95.

* Fourth grade in most countries; see Table 2 for information about the grades tested in each country.

● Percent of total possible points on each item averaged over students.

▾ Average of percentage scores across items; all items weighted equally.

† Met guidelines for sample participation rates only after replacement schools were included (see Appendix A for details)

1 School-level exclusions for performance assessment exceed 25% of the National Desired Population (see Table A.3).

() Standard errors appear in parentheses. Because results are rounded to the nearest whole number, some totals may appear inconsistent.

In the Calculator task, students were provided with a calculator and asked to use it to perform multiplications to explore a number pattern. The numbers to be multiplied – 34 x 34, 334 x 334, and 3334 x 3334 – were such as to yield a clear and interesting pattern in the products. At eighth-grade, students also were asked to work on factoring a given number. The task was intended to measure a student's ability to use the calculator for multiplication, to analyze a pattern in the results, to make predictions from the pattern found, to explain the basis for the predictions, and (at the eighth-grade level) to use prior knowledge of number properties to find factors for a given number. Solving the factoring problem, in which students were asked to find two factors of 455 such that both factors were two-digit numbers and were less than 50, required some knowledge of number properties and was greatly facilitated if students understood the concept of prime factors. Figure 1.15 shows the task with sample responses to all seven items, and the scoring criteria for fully-correct responses. The task was identical for both grades, except that the fourth-grade students were not given the factoring problem.

Eighth-grade students almost universally were able to use the calculator to carry out the required multiplications (Table 1.17, Item 1 – average percentage score: 97%), but they were much less successful in describing the underlying pattern (Item 2 – average percentage score: 40%). Interestingly, despite rather low performance on the description item, students were generally successful in applying the pattern to solve a routine problem. That is, they predicted the next number in the sequence (Item 3 – average percentage score: 75%). This coincides with the commonsense notion that students' ability to understand and to apply their knowledge generally exceeds their ability to describe what it is they know. Eighth graders were less successful in applying the pattern to a less routine situation, i.e., predicting a number further out in the sequence (Item 4 – average percentage score: 55%). Errors in this situation tended to involve incomplete pattern analyses. In attempting to explain their predictions (Item 5 – average percentage score: 42%), a substantial number of students simply made a comment that took the explanation for granted; e.g., "They were easy if you found the method."

The two questions on factoring (eighth grade only) addressed content and procedures quite different from those of the previous items, but were grouped with them because the calculator was useful in discovering or verifying factors. Eighth-graders found it moderately difficult to give three reasons why a particular pair of numbers could not be the missing factors (Item 6 – average percentage score for part one: 45%). About one-fifth were able to find the factors themselves (Item 6 – average percentage score for part two: 21%). Of the students not receiving full credit, some showed the correct factors, but omitted evidence of their work; others gave non-integral numbers as the factors, or tried factors at random.

Fourth-grade students also proved accomplished in using the calculator for multiplication (Table 1.18, Item 1 – average percentage score: 92%), and many could use the pattern to predict the next number in the sequence (Item 3 – average percentage score: 52%). However, describing the number pattern, applying it in a less routine situation, and explaining how they made their predictions were generally very difficult for the fourth graders.

CALCULATOR

FIGURE 1.15 - CALCULATOR FULL-TASK EXAMPLE AND SCORING CRITERIA – EIGHTH AND FOURTH GRADES

ITEMS 1 AND 2

CALCULATOR

At this station you should have:

A calculator

Your task:

Use a calculator to help you explore a number pattern, and to find missing numbers.

Before answering the questions read these notes:

When you use the calculator:

• Make sure that you press the correct keys.

• Make sure that you read the display carefully.

1. Use the calculator to find the answers to these multiplications.

34×34 = 1156

334×334 = 11556

3334×3334 = 11115556

2. What do you notice about the multiplications and the pattern of answers?

Everytime, the number being multiplied has an extra 3 at the beginning. The answers all have the same numbers in them. There is always a 6 at the end, the number of 5's in the answer is the number of 3's in the number being multiplied. The number of 1's in the answer increases with each 3 added to the number being multiplied

TASK M2-P2

ITEMS 3, 4, AND 5

3. Now use the pattern to write down what you think the answer will be to the multiplication below WITHOUT using the calculator.

  33334×33334 = 1111155556

4. Now write down what you think the answer will be to the multiplication below WITHOUT using the calculator.

  3333334×3333334 = 11111115555556

5. How did you figure out the answer to questions 3 and 4?

I carried on the patterns I mentioned earlier

Please turn the page.

TASK M2-P2

ITEM 6 (EIGHTH GRADE ONLY)

6. Ramesh tells Alison that he multiplied two whole numbers together using a calculator and the answer was 455, but he's forgotten the numbers. He can remember two things about them:

- both numbers had 2 digits
- both numbers were less than 50

Alison tries several numbers. She began by putting 7 ¥ 64 into the calculator. But Ramesh said, "I can give you at least three reasons why those numbers can't be the ones I used." What were Ramesh's reasons?

a. both number have to be less than 50 — 64 isn't

b. both numbers have 2 digits — 7 doesn't

c. if the answer is 455 then one of the digits has to end in 5

After thinking a bit about the problem, Alison made some more tries and found the two numbers.

- Now you try to find the numbers Alison found.

You may use any method you like. Write down each of your tries here.

15 x 20 = 300
15 x 30 = 450
15 x 31 = 465
35 x 12 = 420
35 x 15 = 525
35 x 13 = 455

TASK M2-P2

CRITERIA FOR FULLY-CORRECT RESPONSE

Item 1 - Use calculator to perform multiplications.
All 3 calculations correct (1156, 111556, 11115556).
Total Possible Points: 3

Item 2 - Identify pattern in answers. i) Identifies a correct pattern. ii) Includes the repetitions of 1, 5, and may include 6. iii) Identifies a relationship between these and the increasing number of digits or the increasing numbers of 3 in the multipliers.
Total Possible Points: 2

Item 3 - Predict answer to first (routine) calculation. Predicts answer based on application of correct pattern (1111155556).
Total Possible Points: 2

Item 4 - Predict answer to second (non-routine) calculation. Predicts answer based on application of correct pattern (11111115555556).
Total Possible Points: 2

Item 5 - Describe strategy for predicting answers. Describes pattern and a correct method of application.
Total Possible Points: 2

Item 6 - Factors of 455. Responses to two parts are scored separately.

List three reasons why Alison's factors are incorrect. Lists 3 of the following, or other correct reasons: 7 is not a two-digit number; 64 is more than 50; 64 is an even number so the product will be even; neither 7 nor 64 is a multiple of 5.
Total Possible Points: 3

Find correct factors. i) Identifies correct factors (35 x 13). ii) Shows use of a systematic method.
Total Possible Points: 2

Table 1.17   Calculator Task: Average Percentage Score on Items – Eighth Grade*

Country	Overall Task Average▼	Average Percentage Scores on Items●						
		Item 1 Perform Calculations	Item 2 Identify Pattern	Item 3 Predict: Routine Application	Item 4 Predict: Non-Routine Application	Item 5 Explain Predictions	Item 6 Factors of 455	
							Reasons Factors Incorrect	Find Correct Factors
		3 Points	2 Points	2 Points	2 Points	2 Points	3 Points	2 Points
⊤⊤ Switzerland	61 (1.6)	99 (0.5)	51 (3.4)	85 (2.8)	64 (3.8)	55 (3.9)	40 (3.6)	33 (3.7)
Singapore	60 (2.8)	98 (0.7)	33 (4.3)	84 (3.3)	64 (5.1)	45 (4.9)	53 (3.4)	45 (4.2)
Canada	60 (1.5)	97 (0.8)	44 (2.7)	86 (2.2)	64 (2.7)	47 (2.8)	50 (2.6)	30 (1.7)
Norway	59 (1.6)	99 (0.5)	44 (2.7)	79 (3.2)	51 (3.2)	46 (3.2)	69 (2.7)	25 (3.2)
New Zealand	55 (1.5)	95 (1.2)	43 (2.5)	78 (2.9)	56 (3.2)	40 (3.2)	47 (2.0)	24 (2.2)
Czech Republic	54 (2.0)	96 (1.7)	45 (3.9)	76 (3.2)	58 (5.0)	45 (3.7)	44 (3.8)	15 (3.4)
Spain	53 (2.1)	98 (0.6)	48 (4.6)	76 (4.0)	53 (5.4)	53 (3.6)	29 (2.6)	12 (2.2)
Sweden	51 (2.3)	95 (1.2)	40 (4.4)	69 (3.7)	52 (3.2)	49 (4.5)	39 (3.9)	10 (2.4)
⊤ Scotland	49 (3.1)	97 (0.7)	44 (4.8)	65 (4.9)	43 (6.0)	45 (4.5)	35 (3.3)	15 (3.3)
Iran, Islamic Rep.	48 (3.7)	96 (2.0)	43 (6.0)	59 (7.0)	54 (7.3)	30 (4.8)	51 (3.5)	6 (3.7)
Cyprus	40 (1.9)	97 (0.8)	24 (3.6)	56 (3.6)	39 (3.9)	19 (2.9)	38 (3.5)	9 (1.9)
Portugal	39 (2.1)	95 (2.0)	23 (3.3)	62 (5.0)	44 (4.7)	26 (2.9)	21 (3.6)	5 (1.3)
Countries Not Satisfying Guidelines for Sample Participation Rates (See Appendix A for Details):								
Australia	59 (1.9)	99 (0.3)	50 (4.6)	86 (2.2)	67 (3.9)	50 (4.3)	36 (2.9)	27 (4.0)
² England	62 (1.4)	98 (0.7)	50 (3.1)	85 (2.9)	59 (4.1)	61 (2.5)	53 (2.4)	29 (2.5)
Netherlands	59 (2.3)	97 (1.0)	37 (3.8)	77 (3.6)	58 (4.5)	42 (3.0)	78 (3.5)	25 (3.4)
United States	56 (1.9)	97 (0.8)	44 (3.5)	79 (3.1)	51 (2.7)	44 (3.4)	54 (3.1)	20 (2.8)
Countries Not Meeting Age/Grade Specifications (See Appendix A for Details):								
Colombia	31 (1.6)	94 (1.7)	20 (2.9)	46 (4.6)	27 (3.4)	10 (1.8)	13 (2.8)	6 (1.9)
³ Romania	66 (2.6)	98 (1.1)	51 (4.4)	82 (4.0)	79 (4.3)	57 (4.8)	48 (3.4)	44 (5.1)
Slovenia	58 (1.6)	99 (0.5)	34 (4.2)	84 (2.4)	68 (3.1)	35 (3.0)	61 (3.5)	23 (3.2)
International Average	54 (0.5)	97 (0.3)	40 (0.9)	75 (0.9)	55 (1.0)	42 (0.8)	45 (0.7)	21 (0.7)

SOURCE: IEA Third International Mathematics and Science Study (TIMSS), 1994-95.

* Eighth grade in most countries; see Table 2 for information about the grades tested in each country.

● Percent of total possible points on each item averaged over students.

▼ Average of percentage scores across items; all items weighted equally.

⊤ Met guidelines for sample participation rates only after replacement schools were included (see Appendix A for details)

1 National Desired Population does not cover all of International Desired Population (see Table A.2) - German-speaking cantons only.

2 National Defined Population covers less than 90 percent of National Desired Population for the main assessment (see Table A.2).

3 School-level exclusions for performance assessment exceed 25% of the National Desired Population (see Table A.2).

() Standard errors appear in parentheses. Because results are rounded to the nearest whole number, some totals may appear inconsistent.

Calculator Task: Average Percentage Score on Items – Fourth Grade* | Table 1.18

Country	Overall Task Average▼	Average Percentage Scores on Items●				
		Item 1 Perform Calculations	Item 2 Identify Pattern	Item 3 Predict: Routine Application	Item 4 Predict: Non-Routine Application	Item 5 Explain Predictions
		3 Points	2 Points	2 Points	2 Points	2 Points
Canada	47 (2.0)	94 (1.3)	22 (2.6)	64 (3.3)	30 (3.1)	24 (2.5)
†† New Zealand	40 (1.7)	94 (1.6)	15 (2.1)	57 (4.4)	23 (2.8)	12 (1.4)
Iran, Islamic Rep.	35 (2.9)	74 (4.5)	14 (3.5)	44 (3.6)	33 (3.6)	11 (2.6)
Portugal	33 (2.0)	95 (0.9)	7 (2.1)	41 (4.4)	14 (3.9)	7 (1.8)
Cyprus	31 (2.5)**	93 (1.8)	5 (2.2)	30 (5.4)	18 (4.6)	- -
Countries Not Satisfying Guidelines for Sample Participation Rates (See Appendix A for Details):						
Australia	43 (2.5)	95 (1.5)	11 (1.7)	62 (4.6)	31 (5.0)	15 (2.4)
Hong Kong	50 (2.5)	94 (1.4)	23 (3.9)	74 (4.6)	46 (5.0)	15 (4.2)
United States	42 (2.2)	95 (0.9)	19 (2.7)	56 (4.1)	23 (3.8)	17 (1.9)
Countries Not Meeting Age/Grade Specifications (See Appendix A for Details):						
Slovenia	37 (1.9)	95 (2.1)	10 (2.4)	44 (5.3)	23 (3.8)	11 (1.5)
International Average	40 (0.8)	92 (0.7)	14 (0.9)	52 (1.5)	27 (1.3)	13 (0.8)

SOURCE: IEA Third International Mathematics and Science Study (TIMSS), 1994-95.

* Fourth grade in most countries; see Table 2 for information about the grades tested in each country.
● Percent of total possible points on each item averaged over students.
▼ Average of percentage scores across items; all items weighted equally.
A dash (-) indicates data are not available. Item 5 was not administered in Cyprus.
**Overall task average includes an estimated average percentage score of 7% for Item 5 based on overall relative country performance and international item difficulty.
† Met guidelines for sample participation rates only after replacement schools were included (see Appendix A for details)
1 School-level exclusions for performance assessment exceed 25% of the National Desired Population (see Table A.3).
() Standard errors appear in parentheses. Because results are rounded to the nearest whole number, some totals may appear inconsistent.

For the Folding and Cutting task, students were given scissors and a number of sheets of paper, and asked to fold and cut the paper so as to duplicate a set of cutout shapes. They were allowed up to three tries to duplicate each shape, but no additional credit was given for fewer attempts. The task was intended to measure understanding of symmetry and spatial relations, and the ability to solve problems in a non-routine situation, i.e., in a spatial context. The task was the same for the fourth and eighth grades, except for an extra item for the eighth-grade students.

Figure 1.16 shows the tasks and sample student responses, together with scoring criteria for fully-correct responses to each item. Items 1, 2, and 3 make use of the same problem (although it is presented in increasing complexity), draw on the same ability, and are coded according to the same rubric. Item 4 (eighth grade only) asks students to draw the lines where the folds would be in order to achieve the shape provided, without actually manipulating the scissors and paper.

In general, eighth-grade students were quite successful in performing the three folding and cutting exercises (Table 1.19, Items 1-3). International average percentage scores on these items were in the 70s. It is perhaps not surprising that international averages for these items do not differ greatly, since they required essentially the same thinking and manipulative skills and addressed a common problem, albeit with varying degrees of complexity. In the fourth item no manipulation was required, but rather students were asked to think about how to fold the paper and to draw lines on the diagram to show where the folds should be. The drop in performance on Item 4 (average percentage score: 53%) compared with the first three items may be due partly to the more complex pattern, but also seems to illustrate the importance of hands-on materials for problem solving among middle-school students.

As might be expected, the fourth-grade students found the cutting and folding tasks more difficult, with average percentage scores in the 30s and 40s (Table 1.20).

FOLDING & CUTTING

FIGURE 1.16 - FOLDING AND CUTTING FULL-TASK EXAMPLE AND SCORING CRITERIA – EIGHTH AND FOURTH GRADES

ITEM 1

FOLDING AND CUTTING

At this station you should have:

9 sheets of paper.
Scissors
An envelope

Your task:

Fold and cut sheets of paper to make shapes which match the patterns given. For each shape you may fold the paper as often as you like, but ONLY ONE straight cut is allowed.

1. Look at shape number 1 below. Fold a sheet of paper as many times as necessary and make ONE STRAIGHT CUT so that when the paper is unfolded it has the same SHAPE as shape number 1. The SIZE of your paper and cutouts do not have to be the same as those shown here. If you are unsuccessful, you may try again with another sheet of paper. You may try this task a total of THREE times.

   • Write number 1 on each sheet of paper you used for this task.

   • Write your first name on each sheet.

Shape 1

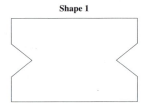

ITEMS 2 AND 3

2. Do the same for shape 2. Remember only ONE STRAIGHT CUT is allowed. You may try this task a total of THREE times.

   • Write the number 2 on each sheet of paper you used for this task.

   • Write your first name on each sheet

Shape 2

3. Do the same for shape 3. Remember only ONE STRAIGHT CUT is allowed. You may try this task a total of THREE times.

   • Write number 3 on each sheet of paper you used for this task.

   • Write your first name on each sheet.

Shape 3

Please turn the page.

ITEM 4 (EIGHTH GRADE ONLY)

4. For this question, shape 4 is drawn below. Instead of folding or cutting shape 4, you are asked to THINK about how to get the pattern by folding a piece of paper and making one straight cut. DON'T FOLD OR CUT ANY PAPER FOR THIS QUESTION.

Instead draw on the diagram below the LINES you would see on a piece of paper that had been folded and cut.

Two copies of shape 4 are drawn here in case you are not satisfied with your first attempt and wish to try again. Remember, only draw lines to show where the paper should be folded.

Shape 4

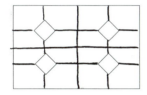

Shape 4

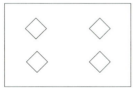

PUT ALL YOUR SHEETS OF PAPER INTO YOUR ENVELOPE, INCLUDING YOUR UNSUCCESSFUL TRIES.

THROW AWAY ANY SCRAPS OF PAPER.

page 3   TASK M3-P2

RESPONSES FOR ITEMS 1, 2, AND 3

1)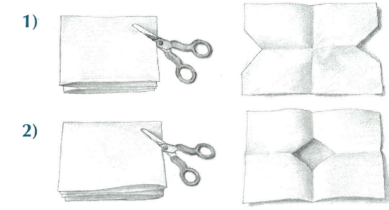

2)

3)

CRITERIA FOR FULLY-CORRECT RESPONSE

Item 1 - Fold paper and cut out shape 1. i) Makes only one cut line. ii) Places two fold lines correctly.
Total Possible Points: 2

Item 2 - Fold paper and cut out shape 2. i) Makes only one cut line. ii) Places two fold lines correctly.
Total Possible Points: 2

Item 3 - Fold paper and cut out shape 3. i) Makes only one cut line. ii) Places four fold lines correctly.
Total Possible Points: 2

Item 4 - Predict and draw fold lines on shape 4. Shows six fold lines in the correct locations.
Total Possible Points: 3

81

Table 1.19 | Folding and Cutting Task: Average Percentage Score on Items - Eighth Grade*

Country	Overall Task Average▼	Average Percentage Scores on Items●			
		Item 1 Fold and Cut Shape 1	Item 2 Fold and Cut Shape 2	Item 3 Fold and Cut Shape 3	Item 4 Predict and Draw Shape 4
		Points 2	Points 2	Points 2	Points 3
Singapore	80 (2.6)	83 (2.3)	86 (2.6)	81 (3.1)	72 (4.0)
Sweden	80 (2.5)	84 (3.0)	88 (2.5)	86 (2.5)	62 (3.4)
†† Switzerland	79 (1.9)	80 (2.8)	89 (1.9)	85 (1.9)	63 (3.4)
New Zealand	75 (2.3)	75 (3.3)	83 (2.6)	77 (2.9)	65 (2.2)
Czech Republic	73 (3.2)	78 (4.0)	84 (2.6)	75 (3.6)	55 (5.0)
Norway	73 (2.1)	76 (3.1)	81 (2.6)	76 (2.9)	59 (2.2)
† Scotland	71 (3.9)	78 (4.2)	80 (4.1)	74 (4.7)	53 (5.1)
Spain	61 (3.1)	62 (3.8)	71 (4.0)	63 (4.4)	50 (4.2)
Canada	59 (2.5)	60 (3.4)	72 (3.2)	63 (3.4)	42 (2.7)
Iran, Islamic Rep.	58 (3.0)	57 (3.4)	69 (3.6)	62 (4.2)	44 (4.0)
Portugal	58 (3.1)	59 (4.2)	71 (4.7)	65 (4.4)	36 (2.5)
Cyprus	48 (2.4)	60 (3.2)	59 (2.9)	45 (2.6)	27 (2.9)
Countries Not Satisfying Guidelines for Sample Participation Rates (See Appendix A for Details):					
Australia	74 (3.3)	76 (3.7)	83 (2.9)	77 (4.4)	59 (4.3)
² England	69 (3.0)	66 (4.1)	80 (3.6)	69 (3.8)	62 (2.9)
Netherlands	71 (2.4)	70 (3.5)	79 (3.6)	75 (3.0)	59 (3.8)
United States	68 (2.0)	72 (2.8)	82 (2.2)	75 (2.1)	45 (3.3)
Countries Not Meeting Age/Grade Specifications (See Appendix A for Details):					
Colombia	43 (5.7)	45 (7.2)	62 (5.0)	41 (7.1)	25 (5.9)
³ Romania	84 (2.3)	89 (2.0)	91 (2.3)	88 (2.7)	67 (5.0)
Slovenia	82 (2.0)	83 (2.9)	90 (1.7)	86 (2.2)	70 (3.2)
International Average	69 (0.7)	71 (0.8)	79 (0.7)	72 (0.8)	53 (0.9)

SOURCE: IEA Third International Mathematics and Science Study (TIMSS), 1994-95.

* Eighth grade in most countries; see Table 2 for information about the grades tested in each country.

● Percent of total possible points on each item averaged over students.

▼ Average of percentage scores across items; all items weighted equally.

† Met guidelines for sample participation rates only after replacement schools were included (see Appendix A for details)

1 National Desired Population does not cover all of International Desired Population (see Table A.2) - German-speaking cantons only.

2 National Defined Population covers less than 90 percent of National Desired Population for the main assessment (see Table A.2).

3 School-level exclusions for performance assessment exceed 25% of the National Desired Population (see Table A.2).

() Standard errors appear in parentheses. Because results are rounded to the nearest whole number, some totals may appear inconsistent.

Folding and Cutting Task: Average Percentage Score on Items – Fourth Grade* | Table 1.20

Country	Overall Task Average▼	Average Percentage Scores on Items●		
		Item 1 Fold and Cut Shape 1 Points 2	Item 2 Fold and Cut Shape 2 Points 2	Item 3 Fold and Cut Shape 3 Points 2
Iran, Islamic Rep.	50 (6.9)	52 (7.1)	50 (6.7)	47 (7.6)
Canada	31 (3.6)	28 (4.2)	36 (4.1)	28 (3.1)
Cyprus	28 (3.4)	33 (3.7)	30 (3.7)	21 (3.8)
↑↑ New Zealand	25 (3.8)	24 (3.5)	29 (4.2)	23 (4.4)
Portugal	21 (3.1)	21 (4.4)	24 (3.6)	17 (2.9)
Countries Not Satisfying Guidelines for Sample Participation Rates (See Appendix A for Details):				
Australia	40 (3.6)	38 (3.6)	49 (4.1)	34 (4.3)
Hong Kong	40 (4.0)	39 (3.5)	46 (5.8)	35 (4.4)
United States	44 (2.5)	42 (3.1)	51 (2.7)	39 (3.3)
Countries Not Meeting Age/Grade Specifications (See Appendix A for Details):				
Slovenia	63 (3.6)	66 (3.7)	67 (4.0)	55 (4.4)
International Average	38 (1.3)	38 (1.4)	42 (1.5)	33 (1.5)

SOURCE: IEA Third International Mathematics and Science Study (TIMSS), 1994-95.

* Fourth grade in most countries; see Table 2 for information about the grades tested in each country.

● Percent of total possible points on each item averaged over students.

▼ Average of percentage scores across items; all items weighted equally.

† Met guidelines for sample participation rates only after replacement schools were included (see Appendix A for details)

1 School-level exclusions for performance assessment exceed 25% of the National Desired Population (see Table A.3).

() Standard errors appear in parentheses. Because results are rounded to the nearest whole number, some totals may appear inconsistent.

For the Around the Bend task students were supplied with a model of a corridor having a right-angle bend, and several pieces of cardboard cut to represent pieces of furniture. The task, in general, was to find out which pieces of furniture would go around the bend in the corridor. The kinds of furniture and their dimensions varied across countries to suit the local contexts. For eighth-grade students, the task was intended to measure the following procedural and cognitive skills: to perform conversions between meters and centimeters; to use a scale to convert model sizes to the dimensions of real-world furniture pieces; to solve a spatial problem by manipulating models; to make judgments about the real-world furniture that the models might reasonably represent; and, finally, to generalize a rule from experimenting with models. The rule needed to relate model width and length to the dimensions of the corridor so that the furniture "would always go around the bend." Figure 1.17 presents the eighth-grade version of the task, together with sample student responses and criteria for fully-correct responses.

The fourth-grade version of the task required essentially the same skills, but involved different models of furniture and different demands for the conversions and judgments about real furniture. For example, at the fourth grade, the first item combined measurement with students' judgment about going around the bend, and so is not directly comparable with the eighth-grade item. The fourth graders also were not asked to find a general rule. Consequently, comparisons cannot be made between performance on items at the two grade levels. The fourth-grade version of the task, together with sample student responses and criteria for fully-correct responses, is shown in Figure 1.18.

Eighth-grade students found the procedural items involving measurement and scale conversion relatively easy (Table 1.21, Item 1 – average percentage score: 84%; Item 2 – average percentage score: 69%). They also had little difficulty in relating models to the real world (Item 3 – average percentage score: 66%) or in identifying which of two pieces of furniture would go "around the bend" (Item 4 – average percentage score: 69%). Drawing models to scale, conjecturing about which real-life pieces of furniture they might represent, and deciding whether they would go around the bend (Item 5) were all more difficult, with average percentage scores in the 40s and 50s. Finding a general rule for predicting from the length and width of a piece of furniture whether or not it would go around the bend proved extremely challenging for almost all students.

Fourth-grade students were more successful in measuring models and in deciding whether they would go around the bend (Table 1.22, Items 1 and 4 – average percentage scores: 57% and 54%, respectively) than in converting from centimeters to meters (Item 2 – average percentage score: 32%) or making models to scale (Item 3 – average percentage score: 33%).

AROUND THE BEND

FIGURE 1.17 - AROUND THE BEND FULL-TASK EXAMPLE AND SCORING CRITERIA – EIGHTH GRADE

INTRODUCTION TO TASK

AROUND THE BEND

At this station you should have:

Two rectangles of white card, A and B, which are models of pieces of furniture
1 cm squared graph paper to make different rectangles to be models of other pieces of furniture
Scissors
A 30 cm ruler
Plastic bag and labels
Paper clips
A model representing a corridor in an apartment

Your task:

Find out what sizes of furniture can be moved around the bend in the corridor.

Read this before answering the questions:

Ray is to move into an apartment which has the main rooms around a bend in the corridor leading from the front door.

What sizes of furniture will go around the bend in the corridor?

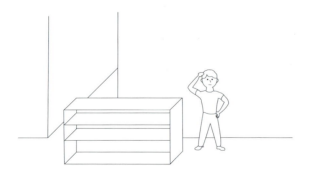

Ray wants to get some large pieces of furniture around the bend the right way up. He does not want to turn the the pieces of furniture on their sides. He uses the models of the corridor and furniture to find out which pieces of furniture will go around the bend.

page 1 TASK M4-P2

ITEMS 1, 2, 3, AND 4

Here are some pictures (not to scale) showing what could happen.

The rectangles representing furniture and the model of the corridor in Ray's apartment are drawn to scale. *Scale: 4 cm represents 1 m.*

1. Measure the lengths and widths of the two models of pieces of furniture in cm.
   A is ___8cm___ cm long and ___4cm___ cm wide.
   B is ___4cm___ cm long and ___2cm___ cm wide.

2. What are the lengths and widths of the two pieces of furniture in meters?
   A is ___2m___ m long and ___1m___ m wide.
   B is ___1m___ m long and ___½m___ m wide.

3. Here is a list of furniture:

   (single bed)   (coffee table)   3-seater couch   armchair
   cot

   double bed   dining table   2-seater couch   sideboard

   Judging from their sizes:
   What piece of furniture is A most likely to be? ___Single bed___
   What piece of furniture is B most likely to be? ___coffee table___

4. Which piece(s) of furniture (A or B or both) will go around the bend in Ray's apartment and which will not?

   piece A will not go around the bend.
   piece B will go around the bend.

Please turn the page.

TASK M4-P2 page 2

ITEMS 5 AND 6

5. Use the graph paper to make other models of pieces of furniture to the sizes listed in the table below. The sizes are all given in meters.

In the second column of the table suggest what the furniture could be.

In the third column find out if the piece of furniture will go around the bend, and check the correct answer.

	Furniture Size		What Furniture could be:	Goes around the bend?		
	Length (m)	Width (m)		Yes, easily	Yes, just	No
C	0.5	0.5	bedside table	✓		
D	1.5	0.5	2 seater couch	✓		
E	2	0.5	3 seater couch		✓	
F	1	1	dining table		✓	
G	1.5	1	double bed			✓
H	2	1	king size bed			✓

6. Whether or not a piece of furniture goes around the bend of Ray's corridor depends on its length and width. Look at the results you have for all the pieces of furniture A, B, C, D, E, F, G and H.

   • Try to find a rule for working out from their lengths and widths whether or not a piece of furniture goes around the bend.

   If the width is half as long as the length it will not go around the bend. But it will if the width & length are the same or if the width is less. It will

PUT THE PIECES OF FURNITURE YOU MADE IN THE PLASTIC BAG AND PUT YOUR NAME ON THE LABEL.

FASTEN THE BAG TO THIS PAGE WITH A PAPER CLIP.

LEAVE THE MODELS A AND B AT THE STATION.

page 3

TASK M4-P2

ITEM 5 RESPONSE

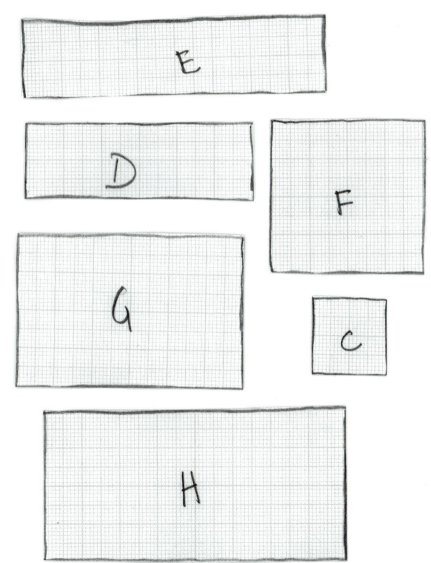

Shown at actual size

FIG. 1.17 (CONT.) AROUND THE BEND – EIGHTH GRADE

CRITERIA FOR FULLY-CORRECT RESPONSE

Item 1 - Measure lengths and widths of two furniture models.
Length and width measured correctly (in cm) for both pieces
(A = 8 cm x 4 cm; B = 4 cm x 2 cm).
Total Possible Points: 2

Item 2 - Convert cm into meters using scale. Computes conversion
of length and width accurately. (A = 2 m x 1 m; B = 1 m x 0.5 m)
Total Possible Points: 2

Item 3 - Relate models to real-world furniture. Judgments are
reasonable for both pieces.
Total Possible Points: 2

**Item 4 - Solve problem: which piece(s) of furniture will go around
the bend.** i) Response is consistent with measurements. ii) Response
is correct (A will not; B will).
Total Possible Points: 2

Item 5 - Draw and make predictions about six models.
Three aspects of responses were scored separately.

> **Draw or cut models to scale.** i) Correctly applies scale.
> ii) Computations and drawings are accurate for all 6 pieces
> (C = 2 cm x 2 cm; D = 6 cm x 2 cm; E = 8 cm x 2 cm;
> F = 4 cm x 4 cm; G = 6 cm x 4 cm; H = 8 cm x 4 cm).
> *Total Possible Points: 3*

> **Relate models to real-world furniture.** Judgments are reasonable
> for all 6 pieces.
> *Total Possible Points: 2*

> **Solve problem: which piece(s) of furniture will go around the
> bend.** Judges all six pieces of furniture correctly, based on
> drawings (C and D – Easily; E and F – Just; G and H – No).
> *Total Possible Points: 3*

**Item 6 - Find a general rule for whether furniture will or will not
go around the bend.** Includes the correct relationship between length
and width based on the corridor dimensions and scale: i.e., furniture
will go around the bend if (1/2 x length + width) ≤ 1.5 m.
Total Possible Points: 3

FIGURE 1.18 - AROUND THE BEND   ITEMS AND SCORING CRITERIA – FOURTH GRADE

AROUND THE BEND

At this station you should have:

Five rectangles of white card which are models of pieces of furniture: a single bed, a coffee table, a dining table, a sideboard, a bookcase
1 cm squared graph paper to make different rectangles to be models of other pieces of furniture
Scissors
A 30 cm ruler
Plastic bag and label
Paper clips
A model of a corridor in an apartment

Your task:

Find out which pieces of furniture can be moved around the bend in the corridor.

Read this before answering the questions:

Ray is to move into an apartment which has the main rooms around a bend in the corridor leading from the front door.

What sizes of furniture will go around the bend in the corridor?

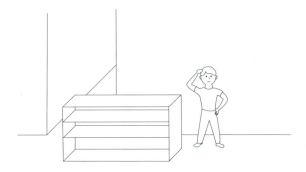

Ray wants to get some large pieces of furniture around the bend the right way up. He does not want to turn the pieces of furniture on their sides. He uses the models of the corridor and furniture to find out which pieces of furniture will go around the bend.

Here are some pictures of the corridor each with a piece of furniture showing what could happen.

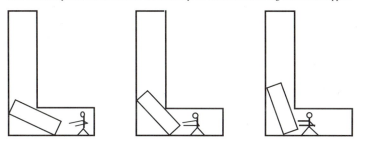

1. Measure the length and width of the model furniture and find which ones will go around the bend in Ray's corridor. Write down what you find in the table below. Place a checkmark in the correct column to indicate whether or not the furniture goes around the bend.

Model Furniture	Length cm	Width cm	Goes Round the Bend		
			Yes easily	Yes barely	No
A. Bookcase					
B. Dining Table					
C. Single Bed					
D. Sideboard					
E. Coffee table					

The models of pieces of furniture and corridor are made to scale: 4 cm on the model represents 1 m on the real furniture.

2. What is the real size of the bed and the bookcase?

The bed is _____m long and _____m wide.

The bookcase is _____m long and _____m wide.

Please turn the page.

FIGURE 1.18 (CONT.) AROUND THE BEND – FOURTH GRADE

3. Ray wants to buy a coffee table measuring 1 m (length) by 1 m (width) and a double bed measuring 2 m (length) by 1 1/2 m (width).

- Use the graph paper to cut out models of these pieces of furniture to scale size.

Remember the scale: 4 cm on the model represents 1 m on real furniture.

4. Draw a circle around the correct words:

The coffee table (**will / will not**) go around the bend.

The double bed (**will / will not**) go around the bend.

- Label the two pieces of furniture "coffee table" and "double bed."

CRITERIA FOR FULLY-CORRECT RESPONSE

Item 1 - For all 5 pieces: measure furniture models and decide whether they will go around the bend. i) Length and width measured correctly (A = 4 cm x 2 cm; B = 6 cm x 6 cm; C = 8 cm x 4 cm; D = 8 cm x 2 cm; E = 6 cm x 4 cm). ii) Judgments about going around the bend are correct (A and E – Easily; D – Barely; B and C – No).
Total Possible Points: 2

Item 2 - Convert cm into meters using scale. Computes conversion of length and width correctly for both pieces. (Bed = 2 m x 1 m; Bookcase = 1 m x 0.5 m)
Total Possible Points: 2

Item 3 - Cut furniture models to scale. Both models are drawn or cut accurately (± 3mm). (Coffee table = 4 cm x 4 cm; Double bed = 8 cm x 6 cm)
Total Possible Points: 2

Item 4 - Solve problem: decide whether furniture will or will not go around the bend. Judges both pieces correctly (Coffee table will just go around; double bed will not).
Total Possible Points: 2

Around the Bend Task: Average Percentage Score on Items - Eighth Grade* | Table 1.21

Country	Overall Task Average▼	Average Percentage Scores on Items●							
		Item 1 Measure Models A and B	Item 2 Convert Using Scale	Item 3 Relate A and B to Real Furniture	Item 4 Solve Problem With A and B	Item 5 Six Models			Item 6 Find General Rule
						Draw Models to Scale	Relate Models to Real Furniture	Solve Problem with Models	
		2 Points	2 Points	2 Points	2 Points	3 Points	2 Points	3 Points	3 Points
Sweden	65 (1.9)	89 (2.1)	95 (2.3)	81 (3.4)	46 (4.4)	70 (4.6)	57 (2.8)	73 (2.7)	12 (2.3)
Singapore	63 (1.5)	94 (1.6)	82 (3.8)	76 (2.9)	89 (2.1)	66 (4.6)	33 (1.7)	64 (2.5)	2 (0.9)
Norway	62 (1.3)	96 (1.4)	80 (2.3)	67 (2.5)	82 (3.4)	54 (3.8)	48 (2.4)	63 (2.5)	7 (0.9)
New Zealand	60 (1.4)	93 (1.0)	74 (2.8)	75 (2.5)	78 (2.5)	52 (3.6)	44 (1.6)	61 (1.8)	3 (0.9)
Czech Republic	58 (1.5)	95 (1.2)	83 (2.8)	61 (3.1)	79 (3.7)	51 (3.4)	44 (2.7)	51 (2.5)	4 (1.5)
† Scotland	58 (2.1)	95 (1.8)	78 (3.7)	50 (3.2)	80 (4.2)	57 (4.8)	39 (3.2)	58 (2.9)	9 (2.6)
†† Switzerland	54 (2.2)	81 (4.5)	80 (4.4)	47 (3.1)	64 (3.1)	58 (5.3)	31 (2.3)	63 (3.1)	9 (1.2)
Canada	53 (2.0)	82 (3.8)	67 (2.7)	63 (3.6)	68 (4.5)	48 (3.7)	42 (2.8)	56 (3.5)	1 (0.7)
Spain	53 (1.9)	90 (2.5)	59 (4.3)	80 (3.3)	72 (3.5)	31 (3.9)	46 (3.3)	44 (3.1)	4 (1.3)
Portugal	43 (1.8)	92 (2.6)	57 (4.4)	60 (3.7)	54 (4.3)	26 (3.9)	22 (2.9)	34 (3.3)	1 (0.4)
Cyprus	42 (1.5)	67 (3.6)	41 (4.3)	60 (2.7)	69 (4.1)	28 (4.4)	31 (3.1)	37 (2.8)	0 ~
Iran, Islamic Rep.	34 (3.2)	69 (4.8)	45 (4.8)	43 (3.0)	42 (8.0)	21 (5.3)	23 (4.6)	27 (5.1)	3 (1.6)
Countries Not Satisfying Guidelines for Sample Participation Rates (See Appendix A for Details):									
Australia	58 (1.8)	84 (3.4)	72 (3.7)	64 (3.2)	85 (2.5)	53 (3.8)	46 (2.6)	61 (3.1)	2 (0.7)
² England	63 (1.5)	94 (1.8)	81 (3.1)	68 (3.0)	82 (2.9)	65 (3.3)	33 (2.2)	67 (2.8)	11 (1.5)
Netherlands	67 (1.9)	92 (1.9)	89 (2.6)	87 (3.5)	80 (3.0)	54 (5.1)	60 (2.9)	68 (2.7)	5 (1.3)
United States	48 (1.8)	68 (3.3)	53 (4.1)	66 (3.0)	62 (3.2)	33 (3.2)	45 (2.2)	52 (2.2)	3 (1.2)
Countries Not Meeting Age/Grade Specifications (See Appendix A for Details):									
Colombia	34 (4.4)**	52 (7.8)	44 (7.7)	56 (6.1)	40 (6.4)	15 (3.8)	37 (4.9)	29 (4.3)	- -
³ Romania	58 (3.1)	79 (5.5)	64 (5.7)	80 (3.3)	71 (4.7)	60 (5.8)	51 (3.5)	53 (3.7)	7 (2.4)
Slovenia	55 (1.9)	82 (3.4)	61 (5.0)	60 (2.5)	79 (3.7)	45 (3.9)	58 (2.9)	52 (3.2)	3 (1.0)
International Average	54 (0.5)	84 (0.8)	69 (0.9)	66 (0.8)	69 (0.9)	47 (1.0)	42 (0.7)	53 (0.7)	5 (0.3)

SOURCE: IEA Third International Mathematics and Science Study (TIMSS), 1994-95.

* Eighth grade in most countries; see Table 2 for information about the grades tested in each country.

● Percent of total possible points on each item averaged over students.

▼ Average of percentage scores across items; all items weighted equally.

A dash (-) indicates data are not available. Item 6 was not administered in Colombia.

**Overall task average includes an estimated average percentage score of 1% for item 6 imputed based on overall relative country performance and international item difficulty.

† Met guidelines for sample participation rates only after replacement schools were included (see Appendix A for details)

¹ National Desired Population does not cover all of International Desired Population (see Table A.2) - German-speaking cantons only.

² National Defined Population covers less than 90 percent of National Desired Population for the main assessment (see Table A.2).

³ School-level exclusions for performance assessment exceed 25% of the National Desired Population (see Table A.2).

A tilde (~) indicates that standard error could not be estimated.

() Standard errors appear in parentheses. Because results are rounded to the nearest whole number, some totals may appear inconsistent.

Table 1.22 Around the Bend Task: Average Percentage Score on Items – Fourth Grade*

Country	Overall Task Average▼	Average Percentage Scores on Items●			
		Item 1 Measure Models	Item 2 Convert Using Scale	Item 3 Draw Models to Scale	Item 4 Solve Problem With Models
		2 Points	2 Points	2 Points	2 Points
Canada	49 (2.3)	65 (2.8)	36 (3.2)	33 (3.4)	62 (2.7)
⁺¹ New Zealand	49 (2.8)	69 (4.3)	30 (3.4)	35 (3.6)	62 (3.3)
Portugal	38 (3.3)	63 (4.4)	32 (4.4)	23 (4.4)	32 (4.2)
Iran, Islamic Rep.	28 (3.6)	42 (5.0)	18 (3.7)	23 (4.9)	27 (3.1)
Cyprus	25 (2.1)	32 (4.3)	7 (2.2)	20 (2.9)	42 (4.9)
Countries Not Satisfying Guidelines for Sample Participation Rates (See Appendix A for Details):					
Australia	51 (4.1)	46 (5.3)	41 (4.3)	47 (5.1)	71 (4.1)
Hong Kong	57 (2.5)	72 (2.9)	45 (5.6)	37 (3.5)	74 (3.0)
United States	42 (2.9)	47 (3.9)	30 (3.7)	31 (3.6)	59 (3.3)
Countries Not Meeting Age/Grade Specifications (See Appendix A for Details):					
Slovenia	57 (2.7)	78 (2.4)	46 (4.0)	44 (3.8)	61 (3.6)
International Average	44 (1.0)	57 (1.3)	32 (1.3)	33 (1.3)	54 (1.2)

SOURCE: IEA Third International Mathematics and Science Study (TIMSS), 1994-95.

* Fourth grade in most countries; see Table 2 for information about the grades tested in each country.

● Percent of total possible points on each item averaged over students.

▼ Average of percentage scores across items; all items weighted equally.

† Met guidelines for sample participation rates only after replacement schools were included (see Appendix A for details)

¹ School-level exclusions for performance assessment exceed 25% of the National Desired Population (see Table A.3).

() Standard errors appear in parentheses. Because results are rounded to the nearest whole number, some totals may appear inconsistent.

The Packaging task involved problem solving in three-dimensional space. Students were supplied with four small plastic balls packed into a square box, some sheets of light cardboard, and an explanation and illustration of a net for the box. With these, and a supply of materials such as a compass, ruler, scissors, adhesive tape, and paper clips, students were to find three other boxes in which the balls could be tightly packed, sketch the boxes, draw a net[4] for each one, and then draw one of the nets to the actual size needed to hold the four balls. The task is intended to measure the students' sense of spatial relations as evident in their ability to visualize different arrangements of objects in boxes, to translate the three-dimensional models first into a two-dimensional sketch, then into the corresponding net, and finally to scale the net to actual size, working from concrete materials rather than by applying a formula to measurements.

The task is the same for both grade levels. The task, together with sample eighth-grade student responses and scoring criteria for fully-correct responses, is shown in Figure 1.19.

As might be expected, eighth-grade students found the task of making and drawing the required boxes moderately difficult (Table 1.23, Item 1 – average percentage score: 53%), but not as difficult as drawing nets (Item 2 – average percentage score: 38%) or drawing a net to scale (Item 3 – average percentage score: 41%). Predictably, the difficulty of the task lay primarily in the net construction, a procedure that may not be emphasized in all curricula. A sample of a net was provided, but in drawing their own nets pupils had to refer continually to their three-dimensional boxes to be sure that all sides were in the right places. Even if they have been taught how, creating a net or projection can be a complex procedure for eighth-grade students. Since eighth-grade students had such difficulty drawing nets, it is not surprising, then, that the fourth-grade students did too. As is evident from Table 1.24, the younger students made some headway with the task of making and drawing boxes (Item 1 – average percentage score: 24%), but found the construction of nets generally beyond them (Items 2 and 3 – average percentage scores: 13% and 16% respectively).

PACKAGING

---

[4] A net is defined here as the two-dimensional pattern that when folded up would yield the three-dimensional object.

FIGURE 1.19 - PACKAGING FULL-TASK EXAMPLE AND SCORING CRITERIA – EIGHTH AND FOURTH GRADES

INTRODUCTION TO TASK

PACKAGING

At this station you should have:

4 plastic balls packed in a square shaped box
Blu-tac to stop the balls from rolling around
Some thin card to make a package for the balls
A compass
A 30 cm ruler
Two pieces of thick card to help measure the balls
Scissors
Sellotape
Paperclips

Your task:

Design different boxes which will just hold 4 plastic balls.

Read this before answering the questions:

The following shows what is meant by the net of a box.

This box has a bottom and 4 sides.

The sides can be cut out separately:

| Bottom |

1	2
3	4

Or the sides can be cut out in one piece and then folded along the dotted lines like this:

This is a net of a box.

TASK M5-P2

ITEM 1

This is the shape of a net of a box like the one that holds the 4 balls. It is not drawn to size but if it were, you could fold up the sides and make the box.

You have been given the box with the four balls just fitting in like this.

Other boxes with different shapes could be made so that the 4 balls would just fit in.

1. Use the balls to find 3 other boxes in which the 4 balls will just fit. Make a drawing of each box with the 4 balls in it.

①   ② ③

Please turn the page.

ITEMS 2 AND 3

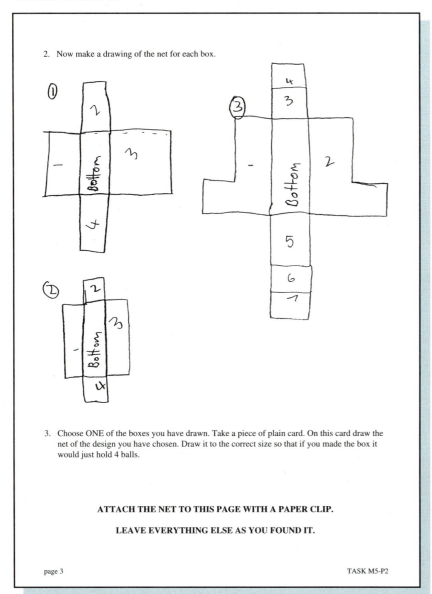

2. Now make a drawing of the net for each box.

3. Choose ONE of the boxes you have drawn. Take a piece of plain card. On this card draw the net of the design you have chosen. Draw it to the correct size so that if you made the box it would just hold 4 balls.

ATTACH THE NET TO THIS PAGE WITH A PAPER CLIP.

LEAVE EVERYTHING ELSE AS YOU FOUND IT.

page 3   TASK M5-P2

RESPONSE FOR ITEM 3

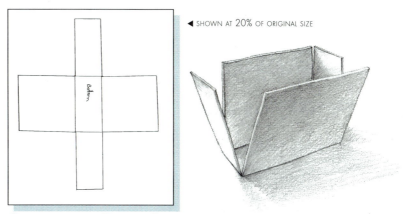

◄ SHOWN AT 20% OF ORIGINAL SIZE

CRITERIA FOR FULLY-CORRECT RESPONSE

Item 1 - Draw three boxes that hold four balls in a "tightly packed" arrangement. i) Each box describes or shows all four balls. ii) Shows balls in "tightly packed" arrangements. iii) Draws at least two unique arrangements.
Total Possible Points: 2

Item 2 - Draw net for each box. i) Nets drawn are consistent with at least two of the ball arrangements. ii) Nets clearly show correct shape of base of box and side flaps required to constrain the balls in "tightly packed" arrangements. iii) Nets show side flaps and base of box in correct proportions (not necessarily in actual size).
Total Possible Points: 2

Item 3 - Construct net to scale. Constructs or draws a net for a box with the following requirements: i) Net is consistent with one of the previous nets drawn. ii) Is constructed out of a single piece of cardboard or pieces are taped together and spread out into a net. iii) Includes base and side flaps that will constrain the balls in the "tightly packed" arrangement when folded up into a box. iv) Dimensions of base and sideflaps are within 4 mm of actual size required to hold the 4 balls.
Total Possible Points: 2

Table 1.23 | Packaging Task: Average Percentage Score on Items – Eighth Grade*

Country	Overall Task Average▼	Average Percentage Scores on Items●		
		Item 1 Draw Boxes 2 Points	Item 2 Draw Nets 2 Points	Item 3 Construct Net to Scale 2 Points
Singapore	65 (2.4)	87 (2.7)	55 (3.8)	51 (3.6)
Norway	59 (2.4)	78 (2.8)	48 (2.8)	51 (3.7)
Canada	57 (3.2)	67 (4.5)	52 (3.7)	51 (4.2)
† Scotland	51 (3.9)	59 (4.9)	41 (5.1)	54 (4.0)
†† Switzerland	47 (3.3)	50 (4.8)	56 (3.8)	35 (4.4)
Sweden	47 (2.3)	68 (4.2)	32 (2.6)	40 (3.7)
New Zealand	44 (2.5)	59 (3.5)	38 (3.2)	34 (2.8)
Czech Republic	43 (4.6)	53 (5.4)	39 (4.1)	38 (5.3)
Iran, Islamic Rep.	43 (5.0)	39 (7.0)	23 (4.4)	67 (5.1)
Portugal	31 (3.2)	35 (4.6)	26 (3.3)	31 (3.8)
Spain	28 (2.3)	28 (3.5)	18 (2.6)	40 (3.5)
Cyprus	14 (2.1)	12 (3.0)	10 (2.2)	19 (3.8)
Countries Not Satisfying Guidelines for Sample Participation Rates (See Appendix A for Details):				
Australia	55 (2.8)	70 (4.2)	57 (3.2)	38 (3.7)
² England	53 (2.5)	72 (3.2)	44 (2.8)	45 (3.3)
Netherlands	53 (2.9)	64 (3.7)	52 (3.0)	43 (4.1)
United States	28 (2.5)	41 (3.3)	27 (3.3)	17 (2.4)
Countries Not Meeting Age/Grade Specifications (See Appendix A for Details):				
Colombia	20 (3.0)	25 (5.0)	10 (2.4)	26 (3.7)
³ Romania	51 (4.1)	48 (4.9)	45 (5.5)	59 (6.6)
Slovenia	45 (3.8)	48 (3.9)	41 (4.0)	47 (5.4)
International Average	44 (0.7)	53 (1.0)	38 (0.8)	41 (1.0)

SOURCE: IEA Third International Mathematics and Science Study (TIMSS), 1994-95.

* Eighth grade in most countries; see Table 2 for information about the grades tested in each country.

● Percent of total possible points on each item averaged over students.

▼ Average of percentage scores across items; all items weighted equally.

† Met guidelines for sample participation rates only after replacement schools were included (see Appendix A for details)

1 National Desired Population does not cover all of International Desired Population (see Table A.2) - German-speaking cantons only.

2 National Defined Population covers less than 90 percent of National Desired Population for the main assessment (see Table A.2).

3 School-level exclusions for performance assessment exceed 25% of the National Desired Population (see Table A.2).

() Standard errors appear in parentheses. Because results are rounded to the nearest whole number, some totals may appear inconsistent.

Packaging Task: Average Percentage Score on Items – Fourth Grade* | Table 1.24

Country	Overall Task Average▼	Average Percentage Scores on Items●		
		Item 1 Draw Boxes	Item 2 Draw Nets	Item 3 Construct Net to Scale
		2 Points	2 Points	2 Points
Iran, Islamic Rep.	34 (5.2)	28 (6.2)	24 (4.7)	49 (6.0)
Canada	27 (2.2)	38 (3.1)	23 (2.4)	21 (2.4)
†† New Zealand	14 (2.2)	22 (3.1)	10 (2.1)	10 (2.4)
Portugal	8 (1.8)	11 (3.0)	5 (1.7)	7 (2.5)
Cyprus	4 (1.3)	7 (2.7)	2 (1.2)	2 (1.5)
Countries Not Satisfying Guidelines for Sample Participation Rates (See Appendix A for Details):				
Australia	24 (2.0)	39 (3.8)	20 (3.1)	12 (2.3)
Hong Kong	15 (2.4)	14 (2.4)	11 (2.6)	20 (6.9)
United States	13 (1.7)	20 (2.2)	9 (2.0)	10 (2.1)
Countries Not Meeting Age/Grade Specifications (See Appendix A for Details):				
Slovenia	18 (2.4)	32 (4.2)	13 (2.1)	9 (2.7)
International Average	17 (0.9)	24 (1.2)	13 (0.9)	16 (1.2)

SOURCE: IEA Third International Mathematics and Science Study (TIMSS), 1994-95.

* Fourth grade in most countries; see Table 2 for information about the grades tested in each country.

● Percent of total possible points on each item averaged over students.

▼ Average of percentage scores across items; all items weighted equally.

† Met guidelines for sample participation rates only after replacement schools were included (see Appendix A for details)

1 School-level exclusions for performance assessment exceed 25% of the National Desired Population (see Table A.3).

() Standard errors appear in parentheses. Because results are rounded to the nearest whole number, some totals may appear inconsistent.

SUMMARY

It is clear from the results presented in this chapter that students generally performed well on procedural tasks involving measurement, use of equipment, and routine problem solving, although naturally the level of success in these areas varied with the task context, familiarity, and degree of difficulty. However, both middle- and primary-school students often had serious difficulty providing descriptions of procedures or trends, and especially in explaining findings and deriving general rules for summarizing results. It is probable that describing and explaining knowledge is inherently more difficult than simply knowing something or applying that knowledge. However, most items requiring explanations in the TIMSS performance assessment were designed to elicit conceptual knowledge wherever present, so some of the difficulty with these items may be due to cross-country variation in curricular emphasis. Pedagogical approach could also be a factor, of course, since in some classrooms students are routinely required to justify their answers and explain their thinking, rather than simply supplying right or wrong answers.

Chapter 2

INTERNATIONAL STUDENT ACHIEVEMENT

OVERALL DIFFERENCES IN ACHIEVEMENT ON THE PERFORMANCE ASSESSMENT

This chapter presents summary results on the performance assessment by showing the averages across the task-by-task results for each country, as well as the averages by subject area and by gender. Table 2.1 summarizes the results for the eighth grade, showing the overall average across tasks for each country as well as the average percentage scores across the items within each task. The average percentage scores for each task are the same as those presented in Chapter 1, accumulated here for ease of reference and comparison. The overall average of the average percentage scores across the tasks reflects equal weighting for each task, even though the number of items within the tasks varied.

The overall averages, shown in the first column of Table 2.1, reveal substantial differences in overall performance between the top- and bottom-performing countries, although most countries performed somewhere in the middle ranges. Also, for the most part, differences in performance between one country and the next higher- and lower-performing countries were relatively small. This pattern of results is similar to that obtained in the written assessment. The relative standing of countries was somewhat similar between the written assessment and the performance assessment, even though relative standings shifted for many countries in the middle range of performance.[1]

Perhaps more important, as shown by the international averages in the bottom row of the Table 2.1, the results also show considerable variation in the difficulty of the tasks. Across countries, the Magnets task was the least difficult (international average 90%) and the Shadows task the most difficult (international average 35%). Because of this wide range in difficulty, the performance assessment results are most useful from the perspective of profiling the strengths and weaknesses of each country on particular tasks rather than simply looking at the overall average. This profiling, however, should be done with care, because the difficult tasks tended to be relatively difficult for students in all countries, and so the international averages for the tasks should be taken into account. Also, because countries that did well overall generally also did relatively better than other countries on each of the tasks, the profiling should be done in view of a country's overall performance. As an example, Sweden performed just slightly above the international average overall, but did particularly well on the Shadows, Plasticine, Folding and Cutting, and Around the Bend tasks compared with the international averages for those tasks.

Table 2.2 presents the corresponding overall and task achievement for the countries participating at the fourth grade. Here, with a smaller set of countries, the range in task difficulty was much larger than the differences in overall performance across countries. At the fourth grade, the Magnets task was the least difficult (international average 72%) and the Packaging task was the most difficult (international average 17%).

---

[1] Beaton, A.E., Mullis, I.V.S., Martin, M.O., Gonzalez, E.J., Kelly, D.L., and Smith, T.A. (1996). *Mathematics Achievement in the Middle School Years: IEA's Third International Mathematics and Science Study (TIMSS)*. Chestnut Hill, MA: Boston College.

Beaton, A.E., Martin, M.O., Mullis, I.V.S., Gonzalez, E.J., Smith, T.A., and Kelly, D.L. (1996). *Science Achievement in the Middle School Years: IEA's Third International Mathematics and Science Study (TIMSS)*. Chestnut Hill, MA: Boston College.

Tables 2.3 and 2.4 display overall averages separately for the mathematics and science tasks for the eighth and fourth grades, respectively.[2] Interestingly, at the eighth grade the international averages for the two subject areas are nearly identical, reflecting nearly equal difficulty levels for the two sets of tasks. The pattern of similar results for the two areas also held for most countries.

As previously explained, with the exception of the Magnets, Batteries, Dice, and Packaging tasks, the items in the fourth-grade tasks differed somewhat from those in the counterpart eighth-grade tasks. At the fourth grade, the science tasks were somewhat less difficult overall than the mathematics tasks (international average 43% compared with 36%). This pattern was reflected in the performance of all countries except Iran. It is likely that the fourth-grade science tasks were simply easier than the mathematics tasks, because as the teachers of the fourth graders in most of the TIMSS countries, including the countries that participated in the performance assessment, reported, students received more instructional time in mathematics than in science (sometimes more than twice as much). From another perspective, however, it may be that in elementary school "hands-on" approaches are more likely to be used in science than in mathematics.

[2] For the purposes of analyzing performance in science and mathematics, the two combination tasks were included in only one primary content area average. The Shadows task was included in the science average, and the Plasticine task was included in the mathematics average.

Table 2.1

Average Percentage Scores Overall and on Performance Assessment Tasks Eighth Grade*

Country	Overall Average▼	Average Percentage Scores on Tasks●											
		Science Tasks					Combination Tasks		Mathematics Tasks				
		Pulse	Magnets	Batteries	Rubber Band	Solutions	Shadows	Plasticine	Dice	Calculator	Folding and Cutting	Around Bend	Packaging
Singapore	71 (1.7)	60 (2.7)	95 (0.9)	79 (2.1)	80 (1.5)	68 (2.7)	50 (3.5)	66 (3.3)	84 (1.6)	60 (2.8)	80 (2.6)	63 (1.5)	65 (2.5)
¹¹ Switzerland	65 (1.2)	51 (1.9)	97 (1.2)	75 (2.1)	67 (1.9)	57 (1.9)	41 (2.1)	73 (2.1)	79 (1.4)	61 (1.6)	79 (1.9)	54 (2.2)	47 (3.3)
Sweden	64 (1.2)	45 (2.6)	95 (1.6)	71 (2.9)	70 (2.4)	50 (2.2)	45 (1.9)	72 (2.9)	74 (2.4)	51 (2.3)	80 (2.5)	65 (1.9)	47 (2.3)
† Scotland	62 (1.7)	55 (2.9)	98 (0.9)	68 (2.4)	75 (1.8)	51 (2.3)	36 (2.4)	61 (2.5)	76 (1.6)	49 (3.1)	71 (3.9)	58 (2.1)	51 (3.9)
Norway	62 (0.8)	48 (1.6)	91 (2.0)	67 (1.7)	63 (1.9)	42 (1.8)	39 (2.0)	67 (2.3)	72 (1.9)	59 (1.6)	73 (2.1)	62 (1.3)	59 (2.4)
Czech Republic	61 (1.3)	46 (2.9)	86 (2.3)	66 (2.8)	65 (3.6)	59 (2.3)	37 (1.9)	68 (2.6)	73 (2.5)	54 (2.0)	73 (3.2)	58 (1.5)	43 (4.6)
Canada	60 (1.3)	46 (2.4)	92 (1.5)	62 (2.1)	71 (2.0)	48 (2.1)	35 (1.6)	65 (1.9)	77 (1.8)	60 (1.5)	59 (2.5)	53 (2.0)	57 (3.2)
New Zealand	60 (1.4)	44 (2.1)	93 (1.6)	68 (1.6)	65 (1.8)	48 (2.1)	29 (2.0)	63 (2.2)	73 (1.2)	55 (1.6)	75 (2.3)	60 (1.4)	44 (2.5)
Spain	54 (0.8)	36 (2.1)	96 (1.4)	73 (1.7)	51 (2.0)	41 (2.3)	36 (1.7)	45 (2.5)	73 (2.2)	53 (2.1)	61 (3.1)	53 (1.9)	28 (2.3)
Iran, Islamic Rep.	52 (2.0)	55 (4.5)	45 (4.9)	52 (4.0)	56 (5.4)	50 (3.5)	43 (1.5)	81 (2.6)	58 (1.8)	48 (3.7)	58 (2.9)	34 (3.2)	43 (5.0)
Portugal	47 (1.1)	24 (2.5)	94 (1.6)	50 (2.2)	51 (2.3)	36 (2.4)	25 (1.5)	41 (2.5)	76 (1.8)	39 (2.1)	58 (3.1)	43 (1.8)	31 (3.2)
Cyprus	46 (1.0)	33 (2.1)	86 (2.3)	66 (2.2)	59 (2.3)	29 (2.9)	18 (1.5)	52 (2.4)	68 (2.2)	40 (1.9)	48 (2.4)	42 (1.5)	14 (2.1)
Countries Not Satisfying Guidelines for Sample Participation Rates (See Appendix A for Details):													
Australia	65 (1.2)	54 (2.6)	92 (1.4)	71 (1.8)	64 (2.4)	59 (2.2)	36 (1.9)	73 (2.9)	78 (2.4)	59 (1.9)	74 (3.3)	58 (1.8)	55 (2.8)
² England	67 (0.9)	59 (2.2)	99 (0.6)	77 (2.0)	79 (1.4)	68 (2.1)	46 (2.3)	55 (2.4)	79 (1.6)	62 (1.4)	69 (3.1)	63 (1.5)	53 (2.5)
Netherlands	60 (1.3)	45 (2.6)	94 (2.1)	63 (2.9)	70 (1.9)	43 (2.7)	35 (2.8)	44 (2.5)	76 (2.2)	59 (2.3)	71 (2.4)	67 (1.9)	53 (2.9)
United States	55 (1.3)	50 (2.0)	85 (2.5)	56 (1.9)	63 (2.4)	48 (2.2)	28 (1.9)	53 (2.1)	71 (2.1)	56 (1.9)	68 (2.0)	48 (1.8)	28 (2.5)
Countries Not Meeting Age/Grade Specifications (See Appendix A for Details):													
Colombia	39 (1.8)	11 (1.0)	96 (1.3)	55 (2.2)	40 (3.7)	26 (2.3)	22 (2.5)	41 (2.7)	49 (4.0)	31 (1.6)	43 (5.7)	34 (4.4)	20 (3.0)
³ Romania	62 (1.9)	41 (3.6)	83 (3.5)	75 (2.2)	45 (3.0)	63 (2.6)	36 (2.8)	63 (4.1)	76 (2.3)	66 (2.6)	84 (2.3)	58 (3.1)	51 (4.1)
Slovenia	61 (1.0)	40 (3.2)	92 (1.9)	71 (1.8)	64 (1.7)	49 (2.0)	31 (1.8)	63 (1.9)	78 (1.4)	58 (1.5)	82 (2.0)	55 (1.9)	45 (3.8)
International Average	59 (0.3)	44 (0.6)	90 (0.5)	67 (0.5)	63 (0.6)	49 (0.5)	35 (0.5)	60 (0.6)	73 (0.5)	54 (0.5)	69 (0.7)	54 (0.5)	44 (0.7)

SOURCE: IEA Third International Mathematics and Science Study (TIMSS), 1994-95.

* Eighth grade in most countries; see Table 2 for information about the grades tested in each country.
● Average of percentage scores across items in task: all items weighted equally (see overall task averages in Chapter 1).
▼ Average of percentage scores across tasks; all tasks weighted equally.
† Met guidelines for sample participation rates only after replacement schools were included (see Appendix A for details)
¹ National Desired Population does not cover all of International Desired Population (see Table A.2) - German-speaking cantons only.
² National Defined Population covers less than 90 percent of National Desired Population for the main assessment (see Table A.2).
³ School-level exclusions for performance assessment exceed 25% of the National Desired Population (see Table A.2).
() Standard errors appear in parentheses. Because results are rounded to the nearest whole number, some totals may appear inconsistent.

Average Percentage Scores Overall and on Performance Assessment Tasks Fourth Grade*

Table 2.2

Country	Overall Average▼	Average Percentage Scores on Tasks•											
		Science Tasks					Combination Tasks		Mathematics Tasks				
		Pulse	Magnets	Batteries	Rubber Band	Containers	Shadows	Plasticine	Dice	Calculator	Folding and Cutting	Around Bend	Packaging
Canada	45 (1.3)	36 (1.5)	84 (2.3)	48 (2.0)	55 (1.4)	40 (1.1)	36 (1.7)	43 (1.7)	46 (2.8)	47 (2.0)	31 (3.6)	49 (2.3)	27 (2.2)
†† New Zealand	38 (1.2)	27 (2.1)	84 (2.2)	37 (1.4)	44 (2.3)	33 (1.4)	34 (1.0)	35 (2.0)	39 (2.3)	40 (1.7)	25 (3.8)	49 (2.8)	14 (2.2)
Iran, Islamic Rep.	38 (2.4)	41 (3.3)	42 (5.1)	40 (3.2)	36 (3.3)	30 (3.5)	26 (2.1)	63 (3.3)	34 (2.9)	35 (2.9)	50 (6.9)	28 (3.6)	34 (5.2)
Cyprus	34 (1.4)	38 (3.0)	68 (3.9)	41 (2.2)	45 (3.2)	42 (1.3)	16 (1.6)	30 (2.1)	39 (2.4)	31 (2.5)	28 (3.4)	25 (2.1)	4 (1.3)
Portugal	30 (1.4)	22 (1.8)	74 (3.1)	31 (2.5)	27 (2.2)	26 (1.9)	27 (1.6)	24 (2.3)	28 (2.6)	33 (2.0)	21 (3.1)	38 (3.3)	8 (1.8)
Countries Not Satisfying Guidelines for Sample Participation Rates (See Appendix A for Details):													
Australia	44 (0.9)	38 (2.3)	77 (3.2)	40 (1.9)	52 (2.9)	39 (0.8)	33 (1.6)	40 (2.1)	54 (1.8)	43 (2.5)	40 (3.6)	51 (4.1)	24 (2.0)
Hong Kong	42 (1.4)	39 (2.1)	74 (3.8)	42 (2.0)	43 (2.5)	41 (1.3)	30 (1.6)	23 (1.7)	48 (3.8)	50 (2.5)	40 (4.0)	57 (2.5)	15 (2.4)
United States	41 (0.9)	42 (1.7)	73 (3.0)	38 (2.2)	45 (1.8)	40 (1.1)	33 (1.2)	31 (1.5)	45 (2.4)	42 (2.2)	44 (2.5)	42 (2.9)	13 (1.7)
Countries Not Meeting Age/Grade Specifications (See Appendix A for Details):													
Slovenia	46 (1.3)	39 (2.7)	74 (3.8)	54 (2.0)	51 (1.7)	38 (1.3)	32 (1.8)	46 (2.7)	44 (2.5)	37 (1.9)	63 (3.6)	57 (2.7)	18 (2.4)
International Average	40 (0.5)	36 (0.8)	72 (1.2)	41 (0.7)	44 (0.8)	37 (0.6)	30 (0.5)	37 (0.7)	42 (0.9)	40 (0.8)	38 (1.3)	44 (1.0)	17 (0.9)

SOURCE: IEA Third International Mathematics and Science Study (TIMSS), 1994-95.

* Fourth grade in most countries; see Table 2 for information about the grades tested in each country.

• Average of percentage scores across items in task: all items weighted equally (see overall task averages in Chapter 1).

▼ Average of percentage scores across tasks; all tasks weighted equally.

† Met guidelines for sample participation rates only after replacement schools were included (see Appendix A for details).

¹ School-level exclusions for performance assessment exceed 25% of the National Desired Population (see Table A.3).

() Standard errors appear in parentheses. Because results are rounded to the nearest whole number, some totals may appear inconsistent.

Table 2.3 Average Percentage Scores Overall and by Science and Mathematics Subject Areas Eighth Grade*

Country	Overall Average▼	Average Percentage Scores by Subject Area●	
		Science Tasks	Mathematics Tasks
Singapore	71 (1.7)	72 (1.8)	70 (1.7)
†† Switzerland	65 (1.2)	65 (1.0)	66 (1.5)
Sweden	64 (1.2)	63 (1.5)	65 (1.3)
† Scotland	62 (1.7)	64 (1.5)	61 (2.2)
Norway	62 (0.8)	58 (0.8)	65 (1.1)
Czech Republic	61 (1.3)	60 (1.3)	62 (1.7)
Canada	60 (1.3)	59 (1.3)	62 (1.4)
New Zealand	60 (1.4)	58 (1.5)	62 (1.3)
Spain	54 (0.8)	56 (1.0)	52 (1.1)
Iran, Islamic Rep.	52 (2.0)	50 (2.8)	54 (1.7)
Portugal	47 (1.1)	47 (1.2)	48 (1.3)
Cyprus	46 (1.0)	49 (1.0)	44 (1.2)
Countries Not Satisfying Guidelines for Sample Participation Rates (See Appendix A for Details):			
Australia	65 (1.2)	63 (1.1)	66 (1.5)
2 England	67 (0.9)	71 (0.9)	64 (1.0)
Netherlands	60 (1.3)	58 (1.4)	62 (1.5)
United States	55 (1.3)	55 (1.4)	54 (1.4)
Countries Not Meeting Age/Grade Specifications (See Appendix A for Details):			
Colombia	39 (1.8)	42 (1.4)	37 (2.5)
3 Romania	62 (1.9)	57 (2.0)	66 (2.0)
Slovenia	61 (1.0)	58 (1.1)	64 (1.0)
International Average	59 (0.3)	58 (0.3)	59 (0.4)

SOURCE: IEA Third International Mathematics and Science Study (TIMSS), 1994-95.

* Eighth grade in most countries; see Table 2 for information about the grades tested in each country.

● Average of percentage scores across tasks classified by primary science or mathematics subject area (see Table 2.1). Combination tasks were each included in only one content area average: Shadows in science average; Plasticine in mathematics average.

▼ Average of percentage scores across tasks; all tasks weighted equally.

† Met guidelines for sample participation rates only after replacement schools were included (see Appendix A for details)

1 National Desired Population does not cover all of International Desired Population (see Table A.2) - German-speaking cantons only.

2 National Defined Population covers less than 90 percent of National Desired Population for the main assessment (see Table A.2).

3 School-level exclusions for performance assessment exceed 25% of the National Desired Population (see Table A.2).

() Standard errors appear in parentheses. Because results are rounded to the nearest whole number, some totals may appear inconsistent.

Average Percentage Scores Overall and by Science and Mathematics Subject Areas Fourth Grade*

Table 2.4

Countries	Overall Average▼	Average Percentage Scores by Subject Area●	
		Science Tasks	Mathematics Tasks
Canada	45 (1.3)	50 (1.1)	40 (1.7)
†† New Zealand	38 (1.2)	43 (1.1)	34 (1.5)
Iran, Islamic Rep.	38 (2.4)	36 (2.0)	40 (3.1)
Cyprus	34 (1.4)	42 (1.7)	26 (1.4)
Portugal	30 (1.4)	34 (1.1)	25 (1.9)
Countries Not Satisfying Guidelines for Sample Participation Rates (See Appendix A for Details):			
Australia	44 (0.9)	47 (0.8)	42 (1.4)
Hong Kong	42 (1.4)	45 (1.3)	39 (1.8)
United States	41 (0.9)	45 (0.9)	36 (1.2)
Countries Not Meeting Age/Grade Specifications (See Appendix A for Details):			
Slovenia	46 (1.3)	48 (1.4)	44 (1.6)
International Average	40 (0.5)	43 (0.4)	36 (0.6)

SOURCE: IEA Third International Mathematics and Science Study (TIMSS), 1994-95.

* Fourth Grade in most countries; see Table 2 for information about the grades tested in each country.

● Average of percentage scores across tasks classified by primary science or mathematics subject area (see Table 2.2). Combination tasks were each included in only one content area average: Shadows in science average; Plasticine in mathematics average.

▼ Average of percentage scores across tasks; all tasks weighted equally.

† Met guidelines for sample participation rates only after replacement schools were included (see Appendix A for details).

1 School-level exclusions for performance assessment exceed 25% of the National Desired Population (see Table A.3).

() Standard errors appear in parentheses. Because results are rounded to the nearest whole number, some totals may appear inconsistent.

GENDER DIFFERENCES IN PERFORMANCE ASSESSMENT ACHIEVEMENT

Tables 2.5 and 2.6 show the overall averages and the percentage scores for each task by gender. At both grades for nearly all the countries, girls and boys had approximately the same average achievement both overall and on the individual tasks.

At the eighth grade, there were no significant differences overall in any country, however there were a few significant gender differences noted on individual tasks. In Australia, girls had higher achievement than boys on the Solutions and Dice tasks. Eighth-grade boys in Romania did better than girls on the Around the Bend task, while Swedish girls did better than boys on the Packaging task.

This similarity in performance of the genders is in contrast to the gender difference favoring males at the eighth grade in the written assessment, which was especially prevalent across countries in science.[3] The main survey results for many countries showed eighth-grade boys outperforming girls in earth science, physics, and chemistry; whereas there was little evidence of gender difference on the performance assessment. However, some of the countries that participated in the performance assessment were among those showing few gender differences in science achievement on the written test.

At the fourth grade, in the performance assessment there were no significant differences in overall achievement by gender and virtually none in performance by task. The only significant gender differences in task performance were in Australia, where girls had higher achievement on Plasticine, and in the United States, where boys had higher achievement on Shadows. For the younger students, however, the similar achievement between the genders is more consistent with the findings for the written assessment. For most countries, gender differences on the written assessment were small or essentially nonexistent in mathematics overall.[4] In science, the gender differences on the written assessment were much less pervasive than at the eighth grade.[5]

---

[3] Beaton, A.E., Martin, M.O., Mullis, I.V.S., Gonzalez, E.J., Smith, T.A., and Kelly, D.L. . (1996). *Science Achievement in the Middle School Years: IEA's Third International Mathematics and Science Study (TIMSS).* Chestnut Hill, MA: Boston College.

[4] Mullis, I.V.S., Martin, M.O., Beaton, A.E., Gonzalez, E.J., Kelly, D.L., and Smith, T.A. (1997). *Mathematics Achievement in the Primary School Years: IEA's Third International Mathematics and Science Study (TIMSS).* Chestnut Hill, MA: Boston College.

[5] Martin, M.O., Mullis, I.V.S., Beaton, A.E., Gonzalez, E.J., Smith, T.A., and Kelly, D.L. (1997). *Science Achievement in the Primary School Years: IEA's Third International Mathematics and Science Study (TIMSS).* Chestnut Hill, MA: Boston College.

Table 2.5 — Gender Differences in Average Percentage Scores Overall and on Performance Assessment Tasks - Eighth Grade*

Country	Overall Average▼		Average Percentage Scores on Tasks●											
			Pulse		Magnets		Batteries		Rubber Bands		Solutions		Shadows	
	Boys	Girls	Boys	Girls	Boys	Girls	Boys	Girls	Boys	Girls	Boys	Girls	Boys	Girls
Canada	61 (1.5)	61 (1.3)	45 (2.7)	46 (3.9)	93 (1.6)	91 (2.0)	62 (2.0)	63 (3.3)	69 (3.0)	72 (2.1)	47 (1.9)	52 (3.2)	37 (2.4)	33 (2.3)
Cyprus	47 (1.2)	47 (1.5)	32 (3.2)	35 (2.7)	87 (3.8)	85 (3.7)	71 (2.8)	62 (4.3)	59 (4.2)	61 (2.7)	28 (3.7)	31 (3.1)	19 (2.4)	18 (2.1)
Czech Republic	62 (2.2)	60 (1.2)	48 (4.1)	42 (3.2)	86 (3.4)	86 (2.8)	72 (2.4)	61 (4.5)	63 (4.6)	67 (3.7)	57 (4.9)	62 (4.4)	38 (2.1)	36 (2.8)
Iran, Islamic Rep.	54 (2.9)	50 (2.7)	58 (7.5)	52 (5.0)	51 (5.8)	40 (7.6)	50 (6.2)	54 (4.0)	54 (7.8)	57 (4.1)	48 (3.8)	52 (4.8)	43 (2.4)	43 (2.5)
New Zealand	58 (1.5)	61 (1.5)	40 (2.4)	48 (2.5)	93 (2.3)	93 (2.0)	66 (2.7)	69 (1.4)	65 (2.5)	66 (2.0)	48 (2.7)	49 (2.6)	27 (2.1)	30 (2.5)
Norway	62 (1.2)	61 (1.3)	52 (2.6)	45 (2.5)	93 (2.4)	89 (2.8)	70 (2.2)	65 (2.9)	61 (3.5)	65 (1.8)	39 (2.7)	44 (2.7)	42 (2.4)	37 (2.4)
Portugal	47 (0.9)	48 (1.7)	24 (3.2)	25 (3.4)	95 (1.8)	92 (3.2)	49 (2.4)	52 (4.0)	47 (2.7)	56 (2.9)	36 (2.3)	35 (4.2)	25 (2.5)	25 (1.5)
† Scotland	64 (1.8)	62 (2.0)	57 (4.5)	52 (2.9)	98 (1.2)	97 (1.2)	72 (2.7)	65 (3.5)	78 (1.5)	73 (2.8)	50 (3.0)	54 (2.4)	38 (2.8)	35 (3.7)
Singapore	70 (1.8)	72 (2.1)	57 (2.8)	63 (3.5)	94 (1.5)	96 (1.7)	81 (2.8)	78 (2.8)	78 (1.8)	83 (2.1)	70 (3.4)	66 (3.1)	47 (4.0)	54 (4.3)
Spain	55 (1.4)	53 (0.9)	34 (3.1)	38 (2.6)	98 (1.1)	95 (2.1)	72 (2.5)	74 (2.6)	49 (4.2)	53 (2.6)	43 (3.2)	40 (2.8)	38 (2.1)	35 (2.4)
Sweden	63 (1.4)	63 (1.6)	47 (3.0)	39 (3.7)	95 (1.8)	95 (2.8)	76 (2.3)	63 (4.4)	68 (3.4)	71 (3.1)	51 (2.7)	50 (3.3)	45 (2.8)	45 (3.1)
†† Switzerland	66 (1.9)	64 (1.1)	53 (3.2)	49 (3.0)	98 (1.3)	96 (1.9)	79 (2.2)	70 (2.9)	67 (2.6)	67 (2.7)	57 (3.1)	58 (2.2)	43 (3.2)	40 (2.6)
Countries Not Satisfying Guidelines for Sample Participation Rates (See Appendix A for Details):														
Australia	62 (1.4)	67 (1.2)	49 (3.7)	60 (2.6)	91 (3.3)	92 (2.6)	76 (2.4)	68 (3.5)	60 (3.2)	70 (3.4)	51 (2.3)	▲ 65 (2.6)	36 (3.3)	35 (2.8)
² England	67 (1.6)	68 (1.2)	58 (3.1)	60 (3.4)	99 (1.0)	99 (0.5)	77 (2.7)	77 (3.6)	78 (2.3)	81 (2.2)	64 (3.4)	71 (2.7)	45 (2.9)	47 (3.3)
Netherlands	61 (1.8)	60 (1.5)	49 (3.4)	41 (3.8)	92 (3.6)	97 (2.0)	68 (2.6)	59 (3.8)	68 (2.1)	72 (2.6)	47 (4.0)	40 (2.7)	37 (5.3)	33 (2.5)
United States	54 (1.4)	56 (1.5)	50 (3.0)	50 (2.5)	86 (3.2)	84 (3.2)	54 (2.8)	59 (2.7)	62 (2.5)	64 (3.5)	44 (3.0)	52 (2.7)	29 (2.5)	27 (2.3)
Countries Not Meeting Age/Grade Specifications (See Appendix A for Details):														
Colombia	39 (3.4)	38 (1.6)	12 (1.5)	11 (1.6)	96 (1.4)	95 (1.9)	52 (4.3)	58 (2.8)	36 (5.8)	44 (2.6)	26 (5.4)	26 (2.5)	26 (3.5)	18 (2.8)
³ Romania	62 (2.1)	61 (1.9)	42 (3.9)	40 (4.0)	83 (4.7)	83 (4.5)	76 (2.7)	74 (3.0)	39 (3.0)	49 (3.6)	60 (3.2)	65 (2.9)	39 (3.7)	32 (3.4)
Slovenia	62 (1.2)	59 (1.6)	37 (4.5)	39 (5.1)	95 (2.9)	90 (3.3)	72 (3.0)	70 (3.1)	67 (2.7)	61 (2.4)	49 (3.3)	52 (3.8)	34 (3.8)	29 (2.3)
International Average	59 (0.4)	58 (0.4)	44 (0.8)	44 (0.8)	91 (0.7)	89 (0.7)	68 (0.7)	65 (0.8)	61 (0.8)	▲ 65 (0.7)	48 (0.8)	51 (0.7)	36 (0.7)	34 (0.6)

SOURCE: IEA Third International Mathematics and Science Study (TIMSS), 1994-95.

▲ = Difference from other gender statistically significant at .05 level, adjusted for multiple comparisons across each row

* Eighth grade in most countries; see Table 2 for information about the grades tested in each country.
● Average of percentage scores across items in task: all items weighted equally (see overall task averages in Chapter 1).
▼ Average of percentage scores across tasks; all tasks weighted equally.
† Met guidelines for sample participation rates only after replacement schools were included (see Appendix A for details)
¹ National Desired Population does not cover all of International Desired Population (see Table A.2) - German-speaking cantons only.
² National Defined Population covers less than 90 percent of National Desired Population for the main assessment (see Table A.2).
³ School-level exclusions for performance assessment exceed 25% of the National Desired Population (see Table A.2).
() Standard errors appear in parentheses. Because results are rounded to the nearest whole number, some totals may appear inconsistent.

Gender Differences in Average Percentage Scores Overall and on Performance Assessment Tasks - Eighth Grade* (Continued)

Table 2.5

Country	Average Percentage Scores on Tasks •											
	Plasticine		Dice		Calculator		Folding and Cutting		Around Bend		Packaging	
	Boys	Girls	Boys	Girls	Boys	Girls	Boys	Girls	Boys	Girls	Boys	Girls
Canada	64 (2.5)	65 (1.9)	77 (2.2)	77 (2.5)	59 (2.2)	61 (1.5)	60 (3.0)	58 (3.6)	55 (2.9)	52 (2.1)	60 (4.1)	56 (3.3)
Cyprus	56 (4.0)	48 (3.6)	67 (3.9)	70 (3.0)	42 (3.2)	40 (2.8)	43 (2.9)	55 (4.2)	43 (2.4)	40 (3.1)	13 (2.2)	15 (3.8)
Czech Republic	69 (4.5)	68 (3.2)	71 (3.5)	77 (3.4)	57 (3.6)	52 (3.0)	73 (3.6)	73 (4.2)	57 (2.4)	60 (1.9)	42 (8.3)	35 (4.5)
Iran, Islamic Rep.	87 (2.6)	75 (4.1)	60 (2.2)	57 (3.1)	55 (4.2)	42 (5.4)	64 (2.5)	52 (4.1)	35 (5.4)	33 (2.3)	42 (8.3)	44 (4.0)
New Zealand	60 (3.3)	66 (3.1)	73 (1.7)	74 (2.0)	54 (2.5)	56 (2.0)	76 (3.1)	74 (2.4)	60 (1.7)	61 (1.4)	40 (3.0)	48 (3.5)
Norway	67 (3.0)	66 (3.3)	68 (2.3)	77 (2.5)	58 (2.8)	60 (2.2)	72 (4.2)	73 (3.1)	66 (2.3)	59 (1.8)	59 (3.2)	59 (4.1)
Portugal	41 (3.1)	39 (2.9)	74 (2.7)	79 (2.2)	38 (2.4)	42 (3.1)	61 (3.6)	55 (5.9)	45 (2.4)	41 (2.1)	31 (3.2)	31 (4.5)
† Scotland	62 (2.8)	62 (4.0)	77 (2.5)	75 (2.8)	50 (4.2)	48 (3.9)	72 (5.2)	74 (5.0)	62 (2.3)	56 (3.1)	54 (4.0)	49 (5.8)
Singapore	68 (3.6)	64 (4.5)	84 (2.3)	84 (2.1)	58 (3.1)	63 (4.1)	80 (3.5)	81 (3.2)	67 (1.4)	59 (2.6)	61 (2.9)	69 (3.9)
Spain	49 (2.7)	42 (3.2)	76 (3.1)	71 (3.3)	54 (2.9)	52 (2.9)	62 (5.1)	61 (2.7)	54 (3.1)	53 (1.8)	29 (3.2)	28 (2.9)
Sweden	72 (3.1)	70 (4.1)	71 (3.4)	76 (2.9)	49 (3.6)	51 (2.7)	83 (2.4)	74 (2.9)	65 (2.1)	67 (2.4)	40 (3.2)	▲ 54 (3.0)
†† Switzerland	74 (2.8)	72 (3.0)	76 (2.4)	81 (1.5)	63 (3.3)	60 (1.8)	82 (3.2)	77 (3.4)	55 (3.5)	53 (2.3)	51 (5.8)	44 (3.9)
Countries Not Satisfying Guidelines for Sample Participation Rates (See Appendix A for Details):												
Australia	69 (4.2)	76 (2.7)	72 (3.9)	▲ 85 (1.6)	56 (2.2)	62 (2.2)	73 (3.9)	74 (4.2)	60 (2.4)	57 (2.2)	51 (3.4)	59 (4.2)
² England	56 (2.6)	54 (4.0)	77 (2.9)	81 (1.5)	60 (2.2)	64 (2.6)	71 (3.6)	67 (4.0)	64 (2.2)	61 (2.0)	52 (4.2)	55 (2.9)
Netherlands	43 (4.6)	45 (2.7)	75 (3.6)	77 (1.8)	55 (3.0)	63 (3.4)	70 (5.0)	71 (2.7)	68 (2.7)	66 (2.4)	55 (4.7)	51 (3.5)
United States	51 (3.1)	55 (2.7)	70 (3.2)	73 (2.5)	55 (2.3)	56 (2.3)	67 (2.5)	70 (3.3)	50 (2.3)	46 (2.4)	24 (3.0)	31 (2.9)
Countries Not Meeting Age/Grade Specifications (See Appendix A for Details):												
Colombia	43 (3.5)	40 (3.5)	46 (6.0)	53 (3.8)	32 (2.6)	28 (2.1)	45 (6.3)	40 (7.1)	34 (8.2)	31 (3.6)	24 (4.2)	18 (2.8)
³ Romania	63 (5.0)	63 (4.5)	75 (2.8)	76 (2.9)	67 (3.5)	64 (2.9)	84 (2.5)	84 (3.3)	▲ 65 (2.8)	50 (4.0)	52 (6.1)	49 (3.6)
Slovenia	69 (2.2)	57 (3.5)	78 (2.1)	81 (1.8)	58 (2.3)	58 (2.6)	81 (3.5)	82 (2.9)	55 (3.3)	53 (3.0)	48 (4.9)	42 (3.9)
International Average	61 (0.8)	59 (0.8)	72 (0.7)	▲ 75 (0.6)	54 (0.7)	54 (0.7)	69 (0.9)	68 (0.9)	▲ 56 (0.8)	53 (0.6)	44 (1.0)	44 (0.9)

SOURCE: IEA Third International Mathematics and Science Study (TIMSS), 1994-95.

▲ = Difference from other gender statistically significant at .05 level, adjusted for multiple comparisons across each row

* Eighth grade in most countries; see Table 2 for information about the grades tested in each country.
▼ Average of percentage scores across tasks; all tasks weighted equally.
† Met guidelines for sample participation rates only after replacement schools were included (see Appendix A for details)
¹ National Desired Population does not cover all of International Desired Population (see Table A.2) - German-speaking cantons only.
² National Defined Population covers less than 90 percent of National Desired Population for the main assessment (see Table A.2).
³ School-level exclusions for performance assessment exceed 25% of the National Desired Population (see Table A.2).
() Standard errors appear in parentheses. Because results are rounded to the nearest whole number, some totals may appear inconsistent.

Table 2.6 Gender Differences in Average Percentage Scores Overall and on Performance Assessment Tasks - Fourth Grade*

Country	Overall Average▼		Average Percentage Scores on Tasks●											
			Pulse		Magnets		Batteries		Rubber Bands		Containers		Shadows	
	Boys	Girls	Boys	Girls	Boys	Girls	Boys	Girls	Boys	Girls	Boys	Girls	Boys	Girls
Canada	46 (1.6)	46 (1.3)	38 (2.4)	37 (2.0)	84 (3.0)	86 (3.1)	50 (2.1)	48 (3.3)	55 (2.3)	57 (1.8)	39 (1.9)	41 (1.8)	37 (2.5)	34 (2.3)
Cyprus	36 (1.6)	32 (1.5)	39 (3.2)	38 (3.8)	75 (4.0)	66 (7.1)	45 (3.3)	34 (3.2)	48 (4.3)	41 (3.8)	42 (1.9)	41 (1.8)	17 (2.8)	16 (1.6)
Iran, Islamic Rep.	37 (3.0)	39 (3.1)	39 (4.5)	43 (3.7)	37 (7.8)	46 (6.8)	41 (4.6)	39 (3.1)	41 (4.5)	31 (3.3)	32 (4.0)	27 (5.3)	24 (2.1)	27 (2.9)
†† New Zealand	37 (1.3)	40 (1.4)	27 (2.6)	27 (2.7)	80 (3.1)	89 (3.0)	38 (1.6)	36 (2.3)	42 (2.7)	46 (3.0)	30 (1.7)	36 (1.8)	33 (1.7)	35 (1.7)
Portugal	31 (1.8)	29 (1.6)	27 (2.6)	18 (2.4)	72 (3.9)	75 (4.5)	36 (2.7)	29 (3.3)	31 (4.7)	23 (2.5)	25 (2.6)	27 (2.5)	25 (2.9)	28 (2.0)
Countries Not Satisfying Guidelines for Sample Participation Rates (See Appendix A for Details):														
Australia	44 (1.3)	45 (1.2)	35 (3.4)	42 (2.0)	80 (3.3)	74 (4.6)	39 (2.3)	40 (3.1)	50 (3.8)	53 (3.2)	40 (1.4)	39 (2.0)	34 (1.5)	31 (3.2)
Hong Kong	42 (1.9)	42 (1.7)	42 (2.6)	34 (3.3)	74 (5.0)	73 (5.3)	45 (2.7)	39 (2.5)	43 (3.2)	43 (3.4)	41 (2.0)	41 (2.1)	31 (2.6)	28 (1.8)
United States	42 (1.3)	39 (0.9)	44 (2.3)	40 (2.0)	73 (3.7)	74 (3.4)	41 (3.2)	35 (2.7)	46 (2.6)	43 (2.4)	40 (1.5)	39 (1.3)	▲ 36 (1.7)	30 (1.1)
Countries Not Meeting Age/Grade Specifications (See Appendix A for Details):														
Slovenia	44 (1.9)	47 (1.4)	36 (4.2)	39 (4.6)	72 (5.5)	75 (5.2)	56 (3.2)	52 (3.6)	50 (2.3)	50 (3.1)	39 (2.5)	38 (1.8)	34 (3.0)	34 (2.3)
International Average	40 (0.6)	40 (0.6)	36 (1.1)	35 (1.0)	72 (1.5)	73 (1.7)	▲ 43 (1.0)	39 (1.0)	45 (1.2)	43 (1.0)	37 (0.8)	37 (0.8)	30 (0.8)	29 (0.7)

SOURCE: IEA Third International Mathematics and Science Study (TIMSS), 1994-95.

▲ = Difference from other gender statistically significant at .05 level, adjusted for multiple comparisons across each row

* Fourth grade in most countries; see Table 2 for information about the grades tested in each country.
● Average of percentage scores across items in task: all items weighted equally (see overall task averages in Chapter 1).
▼ Average of percentage scores across tasks; all tasks weighted equally.
† Met guidelines for sample participation rates only after replacement schools were included (see Appendix A for details)
1 School-level exclusions for performance assessment exceed 25% of the National Desired Population (see Table A.3).
() Standard errors appear in parentheses. Because results are rounded to the nearest whole number, some totals may appear inconsistent.

Gender Differences in Average Percentage Scores Overall and on Performance Assessment Tasks - Fourth Grade* (Continued)

Table 2.6

Country	Average Percentage Scores on Tasks●											
	Plasticine		Dice		Calculator		Folding and Cutting		Around Bend		Packaging	
	Boys	Girls	Boys	Girls	Boys	Girls	Boys	Girls	Boys	Girls	Boys	Girls
Canada	43 (2.5)	45 (2.0)	44 (2.9)	48 (3.7)	46 (2.8)	50 (2.3)	35 (4.4)	30 (4.1)	50 (2.9)	49 (2.9)	26 (2.0)	30 (3.3)
Cyprus	33 (2.4)	30 (2.6)	38 (3.4)	42 (5.3)	34 (3.1)	25 (2.5)	32 (5.0)	24 (4.1)	24 (3.0)	26 (1.8)	1 (0.7)	6 (2.4)
Iran, Islamic Rep.	65 (4.0)	60 (4.6)	27 (3.3)	41 (4.6)	35 (4.1)	35 (3.7)	41 (9.5)	59 (8.3)	25 (3.5)	30 (5.7)	35 (6.8)	33 (6.9)
†† New Zealand	34 (2.3)	35 (2.9)	36 (3.8)	43 (2.7)	37 (2.5)	43 (1.7)	24 (4.6)	27 (4.9)	47 (3.9)	50 (3.3)	18 (3.1)	11 (2.0)
Portugal	26 (3.3)	22 (2.0)	31 (4.2)	25 (3.0)	30 (2.7)	36 (2.5)	17 (4.0)	23 (4.3)	42 (4.4)	34 (4.2)	9 (2.0)	7 (3.1)
Countries Not Satisfying Guidelines for Sample Participation Rates (See Appendix A for Details):												
Australia	33 (2.7)	▲ 49 (2.7)	51 (3.3)	55 (3.5)	43 (3.6)	43 (3.2)	42 (3.3)	37 (6.0)	52 (4.8)	51 (5.0)	23 (3.1)	25 (3.1)
Hong Kong	20 (2.5)	27 (2.3)	45 (4.7)	51 (5.5)	51 (4.9)	50 (2.5)	40 (6.6)	41 (5.6)	58 (3.5)	56 (3.0)	13 (2.7)	17 (3.6)
United States	35 (2.1)	28 (1.9)	40 (3.0)	48 (2.9)	42 (2.8)	42 (2.6)	46 (4.0)	42 (3.1)	44 (4.2)	40 (3.3)	15 (2.2)	10 (1.9)
Countries Not Meeting Age/Grade Specifications (See Appendix A for Details):												
Slovenia	43 (3.4)	49 (3.6)	40 (3.3)	49 (3.4)	36 (3.5)	39 (3.7)	52 (4.9)	66 (4.5)	62 (3.7)	56 (3.6)	13 (3.4)	16 (2.7)
International Average	37 (1.0)	38 (1.0)	39 (1.2)	▲ 45 (1.3)	39 (1.1)	40 (0.9)	37 (1.8)	39 (1.7)	45 (1.3)	44 (1.3)	17 (1.1)	17 (1.2)

SOURCE: IEA Third International Mathematics and Science Study (TIMSS), 1994-95.

▲ = Difference from other gender statistically significant at .05 level, adjusted for multiple comparisons across each row

* Fourth grade in most countries; see Table 2 for information about the grades tested in each country.

● Average of percentage scores across items in task: all items weighted equally (see overall task averages in Chapter 1)

† Met guidelines for sample participation rates only after replacement schools were included (see Appendix A for details)

¹ School-level exclusions for performance assessment exceed 25% of the National Desired Population (see Table A.3).

() Standard errors appear in parentheses. Because results are rounded to the nearest whole number, some totals may appear inconsistent.

Chapter

3

STUDENT ACHIEVEMENT IN PERFORMANCE
EXPECTATION CATEGORIES

In TIMSS, the term *performance expectation* is used to describe the many kinds of manipulative and cognitive behaviors and attitudes that a given task might be expected to elicit from students.[1] It includes such behaviors as problem solving or using scientific or mathematical procedures, reasoning and conjecturing, or the ability to plan, conduct, and interpret an investigation. The concept of performance expectation is an important key to all the performance assessment tasks in TIMSS, for each task was constructed to allow these manipulative and cognitive skills to be isolated to some degree and measured. However, because real-world tasks are complex, many such skills are often entangled, and the isolation is rarely total. For example, conducting an investigation requires knowledge of the subject in order to know what data to collect, skills in using the equipment, and the ability to organize that data and identify trends, as well as relate findings to prior knowledge. The concept of performance expectation is one of a functional combination of skills and knowledge that are exhibited in response to the challenge of specific tasks.

Because a number of processes are involved in every performance task, TIMSS has presented performance results first by whole task (Chapter 1), while showing how individual items (each measuring a different performance expectation) contribute to whole-task scores. In this chapter, items are collected across tasks by performance expectations in an effort to identify underlying patterns of strength and weakness in students' skills and competencies.

PERFORMANCE EXPECTATION REPORTING CATEGORIES

Performance of eighth-grade and fourth-grade students was analyzed for the following five science and mathematics performance expectation reporting categories, derived from the performance expectations aspect of the TIMSS curriculum frameworks.

- Scientific Problem Solving and Applying Concept Knowledge

- Using Scientific Procedures

- Scientific Investigating

- Performing Mathematical Procedures

- Problem Solving and Mathematical Reasoning

The three science and two mathematics performance expectations reporting categories and the items that address them are presented in Figure 3.1. For each category, the types of skills and processes required are briefly explained, and the TIMSS performance assessment tasks and items relevant to each category, based on the skills and abilities elicited by the item, are listed. The assignment of items to the categories shown in Figure 3.1 is based on the *primary* performance category associated with each item. In this chapter, student performance in these performance expectation categories is presented for each country and internationally at the eighth and fourth grades. In addition, international average performance on selected example items within subcategories of the broad performance expectation categories is shown for the eighth-grade students.

---

[1] Robitaille, D.F., McKnight, C.C., Schmidt, W.H., Britton, E.D., Raizen, S.A., and Nicol, C. (1993). *TIMSS Monograph No. 1: Curriculum Frameworks for Mathematics and Science.* Vancouver, B.C.: Pacific Educational Press.

Distribution of Performance Assessment Items Across Science and Mathematics Performance Expectation Reporting Categories*

Figure 3.1

Science

Scientific Problem Solving and Applying Concept Knowledge			
Applying scientific principles to solve quantitative problems or develop explanations.			
Eighth Grade		**Fourth Grade**	
• Pulse	Item 3	• Pulse	Item 4
• Batteries	Items 3, 4	• Batteries	Items 3, 4
• Rubber Band	Item 6	• Rubber Band	Item 5
• Solutions	Item 4	• Containers	Items 3, 4, 5
• Shadows	Item 2	• Shadows	Item 6
• Plasticine	Items 2A, B 3A, B 4A, B	• Plasticine	Items 2A, B 3A, B 4A, B

Using Scientific Procedures			
Using apparatus or equipment; conducting routine experimental operations; gathering data; organizing, representing, and interpreting data.			
Eighth Grade		**Fourth Grade**	
• Pulse	Item 1A	• Pulse	Items 1, 2
• Rubber Band	Items 1A, 2, 3	• Rubber Band	Item 2
• Solutions	Item 2B	• Containers	Item 1A
• Shadows	Item 5	• Shadows	Items 1, 2, 3
• Plasticine	Item 1A	• Plasticine	Item 1A

Scientific Investigating			
Designing and conducting investigations; interpreting investigational data; formulating conclusions from investigational data.			
Eighth Grade		**Fourth Grade**	
• Pulse	Items 1B, 2	• Pulse	Item 3
• Magnets	Items 1, 2	• Magnets	Items 1, 2
• Batteries	Items 1, 2	• Batteries	Items 1, 2
• Rubber Band	Items 1B, 4, 5	• Rubber Band	Items 1, 3, 4
• Solutions	Items 1, 2C, 3, 5	• Containers	Item 1B, 2
• Shadows	Items 1, 3, 6	• Shadows	Item 4, 5, 7

SOURCE: IEA Third International Mathematics and Science Study (TIMSS), 1994-95.

Mathematics

Performing Mathematical Procedures			
Using equipment; performing routine procedures; using more complex procedures.			
Eighth Grade		**Fourth Grade**	
• Dice	Items 1, 2, 3, 4, 5A	• Dice	Items 1, 2, 3, 4, 5A
• Calculator	Items 1, 2	• Calculator	Items 1, 2
• Around the Bend	Items 1, 2, 5A	• Around the Bend	Items 2, 3
• Packaging	Items 2, 3	• Packaging	Items 2, 3
• Plasticine	Item 1A	• Plasticine	Item 1A

Problem Solving and Mathematical Reasoning			
Developing strategy; solving problems; predicting; generalizing; conjecturing.			
Eighth Grade		**Fourth Grade**	
• Dice	Item 5B	• Dice	Item 5B
• Calculator	Items 3, 4, 5, 6B	• Calculator	Items 3, 4, 5
• Folding & Cutting	Items 1, 2, 3, 4	• Folding & Cutting	Items 1, 2, 3
• Around the Bend	Items 3, 4, 5B, C, 6	• Around the Bend	Items 1, 4
• Packaging	Item 1	• Packaging	Items 1
• Plasticine	Items 2A, B 3A, B 4A, B	• Plasticine	Items 2A, B 3A, B

* Item assignments are based on the primary science and mathematics performance expectation category associated with each. Two items are not shown that are assigned to a primary performance expectation category of Communicating: Shadows Item 4 (eighth grade) and Plasticine Item 2B (eighth and fourth grades).

SCIENCE PERFORMANCE EXPECTATIONS

Table 3.1 summarizes for the eighth grade in each country, the average percentage score for each of the science performance expectation reporting categories, as well as the overall average percentage scores across all tasks. The overall averages of the percentage scores across the tasks are those presented in Chapter 2; they are included here for ease of reference. The average percentage score for each performance expectation category is based on the percentage score for each item within the category (see Figure 3.1), averaged across all items within the category.[2]

The results presented in Table 3.1 reveal that, for the most part, differences in performance between one country and the next higher- and lower-performing countries were relatively small for each of the science performance expectation categories. Note also that, on average internationally, students performed significantly lower on "Scientific Problem Solving and Applying Concept Knowledge" than in "Using Scientific Procedures" and "Scientific Investigating." Internationally, students performed similarly in the latter two categories, with average percentage scores of about 60% for both, compared to 47% for "Scientific Problem Solving and Applying Concept Knowledge".

Table 3.2 presents the corresponding results for the fourth grade. Although the categories are the same as for the eighth grade, the tasks and items within the categories are not the same because not all tasks and items were parallel (see Figure 3.1). In particular, some questions on problem solving and investigating, which were presented towards the end of the eighth-grade tasks, were not administered to fourth-grade students, and these were among the most problematic for the older students. Similar to the eighth-grade students, the fourth graders found "Scientific Problem Solving and Applying Concept Knowledge" to be the most difficult area, with an international average percentage score of 23%. Internationally and in every country, fourth-grade students performed better in "Using Scientific Procedures" than in the other two categories. The international average percentage score of 58% for this category was comparable to performance in this area at the eighth grade. Internationally, "Scientific Investigating" was intermediate in difficulty for the fourth-grade students, with an average percentage score of 43%.

"Scientific Problem Solving and Applying Concept Knowledge" was the most demanding category in all but one country at both grades. In all but six countries, competence in procedural skills and the higher-order skills involved in scientific investigating was approximately equivalent at the eighth grade. A closer look at the item-level scores in Chapter 1, however, reveals that investigating comprises thinking processes of varying levels of difficulty, ranging from planning and collecting data to interpreting and drawing conclusions. Averages across such diverse processes obscure the difference between conducting investigations and using purely procedural skills. Figures 3.3 and 3.4, discussed later in this chapter, are included to illustrate this point.

---

[2] The percentage score on an item is the score achieved by a student expressed as a percentage of the maximum points available on that item. A country's average percentage score is the average of its students' percentage scores.

Average Percentage Scores by Science Performance Expectation Categories Eighth Grade*   Table 3.1

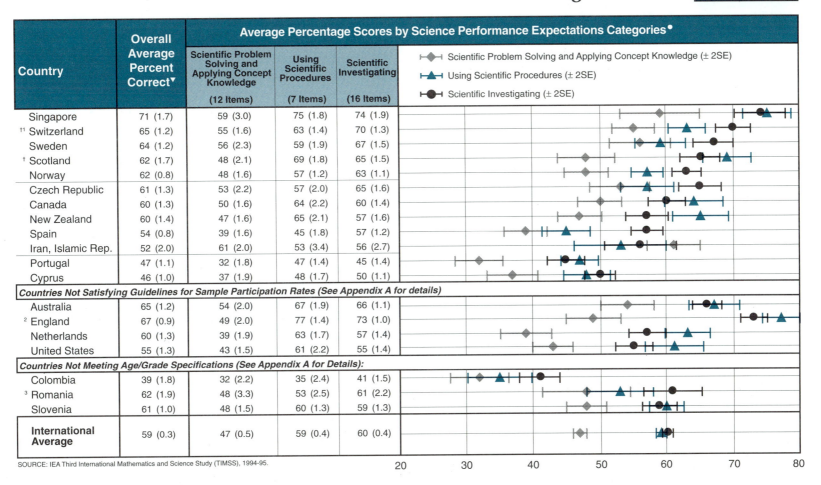

Country	Overall Average Percent Correct▼	Average Percentage Scores by Science Performance Expectations Categories ●		
		Scientific Problem Solving and Applying Concept Knowledge (12 Items)	Using Scientific Procedures (7 Items)	Scientific Investigating (16 Items)
Singapore	71 (1.7)	59 (3.0)	75 (1.8)	74 (1.9)
†1 Switzerland	65 (1.2)	55 (1.6)	63 (1.4)	70 (1.3)
Sweden	64 (1.2)	56 (2.3)	59 (1.9)	67 (1.5)
† Scotland	62 (1.7)	48 (2.1)	69 (1.8)	65 (1.5)
Norway	62 (0.8)	48 (1.6)	57 (1.2)	63 (1.1)
Czech Republic	61 (1.3)	53 (2.2)	57 (2.0)	65 (1.6)
Canada	60 (1.3)	50 (1.6)	64 (2.2)	60 (1.4)
New Zealand	60 (1.4)	47 (1.6)	65 (2.1)	57 (1.6)
Spain	54 (0.8)	39 (1.6)	45 (1.8)	57 (1.2)
Iran, Islamic Rep.	52 (2.0)	61 (2.0)	53 (3.4)	56 (2.7)
Portugal	47 (1.1)	32 (1.8)	47 (1.4)	45 (1.4)
Cyprus	46 (1.0)	37 (1.9)	48 (1.7)	50 (1.1)
Countries Not Satisfying Guidelines for Sample Participation Rates (See Appendix A for details)				
Australia	65 (1.2)	54 (2.0)	67 (1.9)	66 (1.1)
² England	67 (0.9)	49 (2.0)	77 (1.4)	73 (1.0)
Netherlands	60 (1.3)	39 (1.9)	63 (1.7)	57 (1.4)
United States	55 (1.3)	43 (1.5)	61 (2.2)	55 (1.4)
Countries Not Meeting Age/Grade Specifications (See Appendix A for Details):				
Colombia	39 (1.8)	32 (2.2)	35 (2.4)	41 (1.5)
³ Romania	62 (1.9)	48 (3.3)	53 (2.5)	61 (2.2)
Slovenia	61 (1.0)	48 (1.5)	60 (1.3)	59 (1.3)
International Average	59 (0.3)	47 (0.5)	59 (0.4)	60 (0.4)

Legend: ◆ Scientific Problem Solving and Applying Concept Knowledge (± 2SE); ▲ Using Scientific Procedures (± 2SE); ● Scientific Investigating (± 2SE)

SOURCE: IEA Third International Mathematics and Science Study (TIMSS), 1994-95.

* Eighth grade in most countries; see Table 2 for information about the grades tested in each country.

● Percentage scores averaged across items in each performance expectation category (see Figure 3.1); items weighted equally.

▼ Overall average of percentage scores across all 12 performance assessment tasks; tasks weighted equally (see overall average in Table 2.1).

† Met guidelines for sample participation rates only after replacement schools were included (see Appendix A for details)

¹ National Desired Population does not cover all of International Desired Population (see Table A.2) - German-speaking cantons only.

² National Defined Population covers less than 90 percent of National Desired Population for the main assessment (see Table A.2).

³ School-level exclusions for performance assessment exceed 25% of the National Desired Population (see Table A.2).

() Standard errors appear in parentheses. Because results are rounded to the nearest whole number, some totals or plots may appear inconsistent.

Table 3.2 — Average Percentage Scores by Science Performance Expectation Categories Fourth Grade*

Country	Average of Percentage Scores Across All Tasks▼	Average Percentage Scores by Science Performance Expectations Categories●		
		Scientific Problem Solving and Applying Concept Knowledge (14 Items)	Using Scientific Procedures (8 Items)	Scientific Investigating (13 Items)
Canada	45 (1.3)	28 (1.2)	61 (1.4)	53 (1.3)
†† New Zealand	38 (1.2)	20 (0.9)	60 (1.6)	41 (1.4)
Iran, Islamic Rep.	38 (2.4)	34 (2.0)	53 (2.8)	37 (2.0)
Cyprus	34 (1.4)	17 (1.3)	52 (2.3)	45 (1.8)
Portugal	30 (1.4)	13 (1.3)	52 (1.8)	30 (1.5)
Countries Not Satisfying Guidelines for Sample Participation Rates (See Appendix A for Details):				
Australia	44 (0.9)	23 (1.2)	60 (2.5)	49 (1.2)
Hong Kong	42 (1.4)	19 (1.1)	54 (1.7)	46 (1.5)
United States	41 (0.9)	22 (0.8)	63 (1.1)	42 (1.1)
Countries Not Meeting Age/Grade Specifications (See Appendix A for Details):				
Slovenia	46 (1.3)	29 (1.5)	62 (2.2)	48 (1.6)
International Average	40 (0.5)	23 (0.4)	58 (0.7)	43 (0.5)

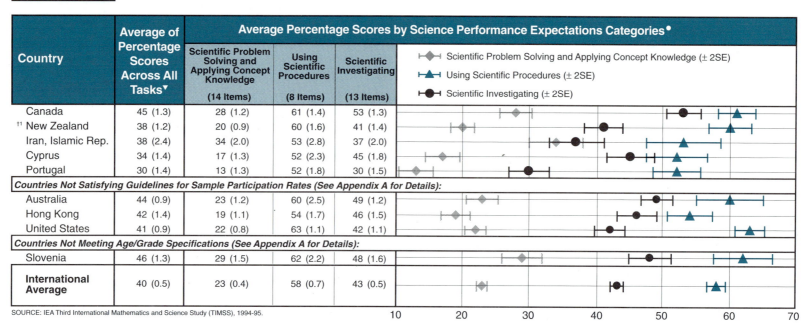

Legend:
◆ Scientific Problem Solving and Applying Concept Knowledge (± 2SE)
▲ Using Scientific Procedures (± 2SE)
● Scientific Investigating (± 2SE)

SOURCE: IEA Third International Mathematics and Science Study (TIMSS), 1994-95.

10   20   30   40   50   60   70

* Fourth grade in most countries; see Table 2 for information about the grades tested in each country.

● Percentage scores averaged across items in each performance expectation category (see Figure 3.1); items weighted equally.

▼ Overall average of percentage scores across all 12 performance assessment tasks; tasks weighted equally (see overall average in Table 2.2).

† Met guidelines for sample participation rates only after replacement schools were included (see Appendix A for details)

1 School-level exclusions for performance assessment exceed 25% of the National Desired Population (see Table A.3).

() Standard errors appear in parentheses. Because results are rounded to the nearest whole number, some totals or plots may appear inconsistent.

MATHEMATICS PERFORMANCE EXPECTATIONS

Table 3.3 summarizes, for the eighth grade, the average percentage score for the two mathematics performance expectation reporting categories as well as the overall average of the percentage scores across all tasks. The latter are the same as those presented in Chapter 2, and, again, they are included here for ease of reference. In all countries and internationally, eighth-grade students performed significantly better in "Performing Mathematical Procedures" than in "Problem Solving and Mathematical Reasoning," with international average percentage scores of 70% and 52% on the items in the two categories, respectively.

Table 3.4 presents the corresponding results for the fourth grade. Again, although the two categories are the same for the fourth and eighth graders, the tasks and items within the categories differ. Internationally, and in most countries, "Problem Solving and Mathematical Reasoning" was also significantly more difficult for fourth-grade students than was "Performing Mathematics Procedures," with corresponding average percentage scores of 43% and 32%. In Iran and Slovenia, however, students performed similarly in the two areas.

Table 3.3 — Average Percentage Scores by Mathematics Performance Expectation Categories Eighth Grade*

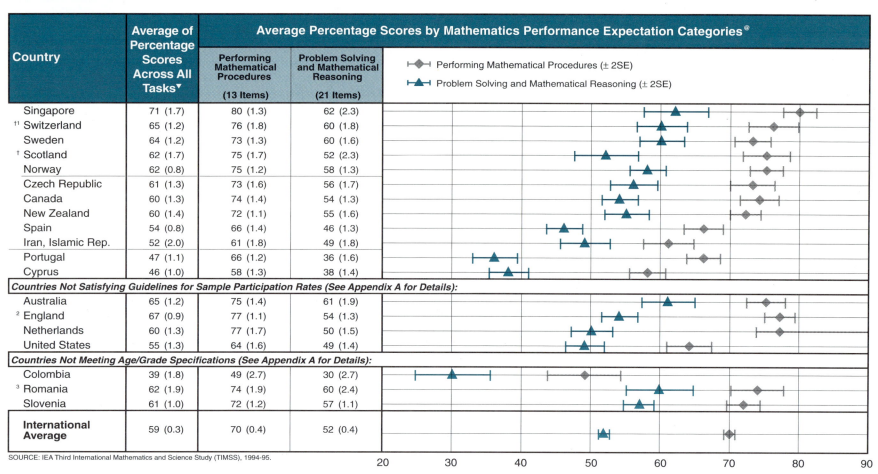

Country	Average of Percentage Scores Across All Tasks▼	Average Percentage Scores by Mathematics Performance Expectation Categories●	
		Performing Mathematical Procedures (13 Items)	Problem Solving and Mathematical Reasoning (21 Items)
Singapore	71 (1.7)	80 (1.3)	62 (2.3)
†† Switzerland	65 (1.2)	76 (1.8)	60 (1.8)
Sweden	64 (1.2)	73 (1.3)	60 (1.6)
† Scotland	62 (1.7)	75 (1.7)	52 (2.3)
Norway	62 (0.8)	75 (1.2)	58 (1.3)
Czech Republic	61 (1.3)	73 (1.6)	56 (1.7)
Canada	60 (1.3)	74 (1.4)	54 (1.3)
New Zealand	60 (1.4)	72 (1.1)	55 (1.6)
Spain	54 (0.8)	66 (1.4)	46 (1.3)
Iran, Islamic Rep.	52 (2.0)	61 (1.8)	49 (1.8)
Portugal	47 (1.1)	66 (1.2)	36 (1.6)
Cyprus	46 (1.0)	58 (1.3)	38 (1.4)
Countries Not Satisfying Guidelines for Sample Participation Rates (See Appendix A for Details):			
Australia	65 (1.2)	75 (1.4)	61 (1.9)
² England	67 (0.9)	77 (1.1)	54 (1.3)
Netherlands	60 (1.3)	77 (1.7)	50 (1.5)
United States	55 (1.3)	64 (1.6)	49 (1.4)
Countries Not Meeting Age/Grade Specifications (See Appendix A for Details):			
Colombia	39 (1.8)	49 (2.7)	30 (2.7)
³ Romania	62 (1.9)	74 (1.9)	60 (2.4)
Slovenia	61 (1.0)	72 (1.2)	57 (1.1)
International Average	59 (0.3)	70 (0.4)	52 (0.4)

Legend: ◆ Performing Mathematical Procedures (± 2SE); ▲ Problem Solving and Mathematical Reasoning (± 2SE)

SOURCE: IEA Third International Mathematics and Science Study (TIMSS), 1994-95.

* Eighth grade in most countries; see Table 2 for information about the grades tested in each country.
● Percentage scores averaged across items in each performance expectation category (see Figure 3.1); items weighted equally.
▼ Overall average of percentage scores across all 12 performance assessment tasks; tasks weighted equally (see overall average in Table 2.1).
† Met guidelines for sample participation rates only after replacement schools were included (see Appendix A for details)
¹ National Desired Population does not cover all of International Desired Population (see Table A.2) - German-speaking cantons only.
² National Defined Population covers less than 90 percent of National Desired Population for the main assessment (see Table A.2).
³ School-level exclusions for performance assessment exceed 25% of the National Desired Population (see Table A.2).
() Standard errors appear in parentheses. Because results are rounded to the nearest whole number, some totals or plots may appear inconsistent.

Average Percentage Scores by Mathematics Performance Expectation Categories Fourth Grade*

Table 3.4

Country	Average of Percentage Scores Across All Tasks▼	Average Percentage Scores by Mathematics Performance Expectation Categories●		
		Performing Mathematical Procedures (12 Items)	Problem Solving and Mathematical Reasoning (16 Items)	
Canada	45 (1.3)	48 (1.9)	36 (1.7)	
†† New Zealand	38 (1.2)	42 (1.8)	29 (1.3)	
Iran, Islamic Rep.	38 (2.4)	40 (2.7)	43 (3.2)	
Cyprus	34 (1.4)	36 (1.4)	22 (1.9)	
Portugal	30 (1.4)	35 (2.0)	18 (2.0)	
Countries Not Satisfying Guidelines for Sample Participation Rates (See Appendix A for Details):				
Australia	44 (0.9)	51 (1.5)	36 (1.6)	
Hong Kong	42 (1.4)	48 (2.8)	32 (1.3)	
United States	41 (0.9)	44 (1.7)	31 (1.2)	
Countries Not Meeting Age/Grade Specifications (See Appendix A for Details):				
Slovenia	46 (1.3)	46 (1.7)	42 (2.0)	
International Average	40 (0.5)	43 (0.7)	32 (0.6)	

Legend: ◆ Performing Mathematical Procedures (± 2SE) ▲ Problem Solving and Mathematical Reasoning (± 2SE)

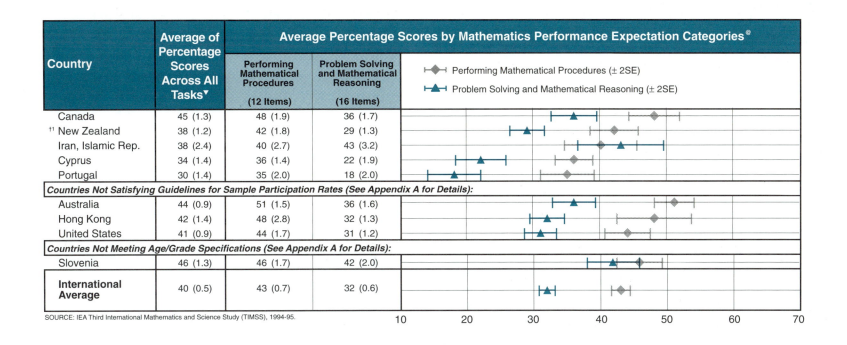

SOURCE: IEA Third International Mathematics and Science Study (TIMSS), 1994-95.

10   20   30   40   50   60   70

* Fourth grade in most countries; see Table 2 for information about the grades tested in each country.

● Percentage scores averaged across items in each performance expectation category (see Figure 3.1); items weighted equally.

▼ Overall average of percentage scores across all 12 performance assessment tasks; tasks weighted equally (see overall average in Table 2.2).

† Met guidelines for sample participation rates only after replacement schools were included (see Appendix A for details)

1 School-level exclusions for performance assessment exceed 25% of the National Desired Population (see Table A.3).

() Standard errors appear in parentheses. Because results are rounded to the nearest whole number, some totals or plots may appear inconsistent.

VARIATION IN PERFORMANCE IN SUBCATEGORIES OF PERFORMANCE EXPECTATIONS

To provide a better picture of the variation in performance across tasks that may be masked by the aggregation of items into broad performance expectation categories, Figures 3.2 through 3.6 present profiles of international performance for eighth graders on items within subcategories of the science and mathematics performance expectation categories. These displays reveal the performance of students in the finer-level cognitive and procedural skills areas contained within the larger categories. For each subcategory, performance on one or more underlying processes or skills is illustrated through several example items, selected to cover a range of item types and tasks. The tasks and items were shown in full in Chapter 1. While previous displays in this report have shown the average percentage scores for items and tasks, Figures 3.2 through 3.6 show the percentage of students, internationally, providing fully-correct and partially-correct responses.

Figure 3.2 presents the percentage of students internationally that provided fully-correct and partially-correct responses to five items from "Scientific Problem Solving and Applying Concept Knowledge," which was the most difficult performance expectation category as shown by the international average percentage score of 47% (see Table 3.1). One of the underlying processes exemplified by many of the items in this category is the application of scientific principles to develop explanations. The performance on these example items shows that students had difficulty in this area across several tasks covering different content areas and experimental contexts. The percentage of students with fully-correct responses on these items varied from 8% to 36%.

Figure 3.3 shows the percentage of students internationally who provided fully- and partially-correct responses to example items in the "Using Scientific Procedures" category. These items measured

students' ability to collect, organize, and represent data, and the performance shown in Figure 3.3 reflects the portion of the item scores based only on the quality of their data presentation (properly labeled tables or graphs showing paired measurements). There was more variation in performance on the items in this category, with percentage of students with fully-correct responses ranging from 17% to 77% across tasks.

Figure 3.4 shows the percentages of fully- and partially-correct responses to example items in "Scientific Investigating" for three subcategories in this performance expectation category. The items in the "Conducting Investigations" category (top panel) are the same as those shown in Figure 3.3. In Figure 3.4, however, the performance indicated reflects the portion of the item score based on the quality of the data collection (making appropriate, sufficient, and plausible measurements). Again, a range of performances is found for these items – 14% to 82% of students internationally with fully-correct responses. For the items in "Interpreting Data" (middle panel), students were required to describe their strategy, interpret their observations, and identify the trends observed in their data. On all of these example items across five tasks, nearly 50% or more of students received full credit. Performance on example items in "Formulating Conclusions" (bottom panel) shows that the relative difficulty of the items in this subcategory varied substantially across tasks. International percentages of fully-correct responses ranged from a high of 92% for identifying the stronger of two magnets to only 16% on the much more challenging task of writing a general rule about shadow sizes.

Profiles of International Performance on Example Items That Require Scientific Problem Solving and Applying Concept Knowledge - Eighth Grade*

Figure 3.2

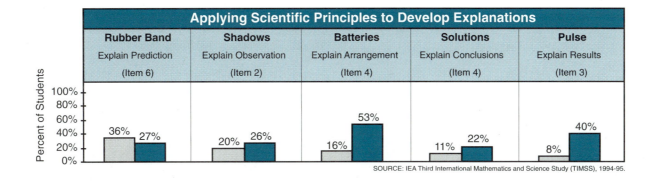

Applying Scientific Principles to Develop Explanations				
Rubber Band	**Shadows**	**Batteries**	**Solutions**	**Pulse**
Explain Prediction	Explain Observation	Explain Arrangement	Explain Conclusions	Explain Results
(Item 6)	(Item 2)	(Item 4)	(Item 4)	(Item 3)

SOURCE: IEA Third International Mathematics and Science Study (TIMSS), 1994-95.

Legend

Percent of Students Internationally with Fully-Correct Response

Percent of Students Internationally with Partially-Correct Response

* Eighth grade in most countries; see Table 2 for information about the grades tested in each country.

Figure 3.3 | Profiles of International Performance on Example Items That Require Using Scientific Procedures - Eighth Grade*

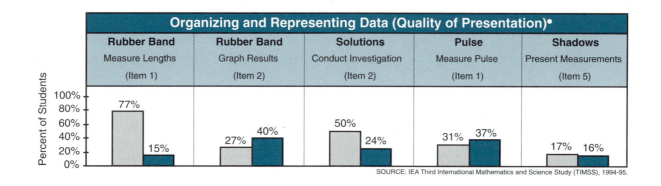

SOURCE: IEA Third International Mathematics and Science Study (TIMSS), 1994-95.

Legend

Percent of Students Internationally with Fully-Correct Response

Percent of Students Internationally with Partially-Correct Response

* Eighth grade in most countries; see Table 2 for information about the grades tested in each country.

• Percent correct reflects only the portion of the item score based on the quality of the data presentation; quality of data collection results are shown in Figure 3.4.

Profiles of International Performance on Example Items That Require Scientific Investigating - Eighth Grade*

Figure 3.4

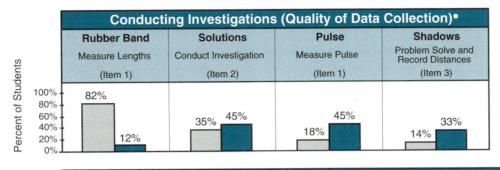

Conducting Investigations (Quality of Data Collection)•

Rubber Band	Solutions	Pulse	Shadows
Measure Lengths	Conduct Investigation	Measure Pulse	Problem Solve and Record Distances
(Item 1)	(Item 2)	(Item 1)	(Item 3)

Percent of Students

- Rubber Band: 82%, 12%
- Solutions: 35%, 45%
- Pulse: 18%, 45%
- Shadows: 14%, 33%

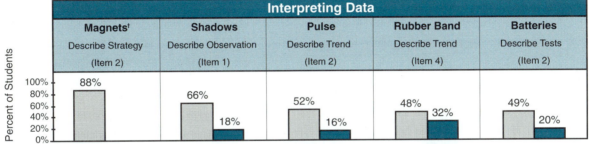

Interpreting Data

Magnets†	Shadows	Pulse	Rubber Band	Batteries
Describe Strategy	Describe Observation	Describe Trend	Describe Trend	Describe Tests
(Item 2)	(Item 1)	(Item 2)	(Item 4)	(Item 2)

Percent of Students

- Magnets: 88%
- Shadows: 66%, 18%
- Pulse: 52%, 16%
- Rubber Band: 48%, 32%
- Batteries: 49%, 20%

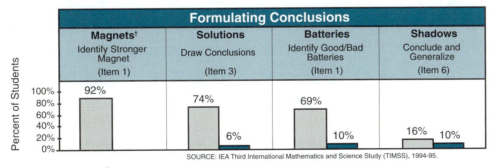

Formulating Conclusions

Magnets†	Solutions	Batteries	Shadows
Identify Stronger Magnet	Draw Conclusions	Identify Good/Bad Batteries	Conclude and Generalize
(Item 1)	(Item 3)	(Item 1)	(Item 6)

Percent of Students

- Magnets: 92%
- Solutions: 74%, 6%
- Batteries: 69%, 10%
- Shadows: 16%, 10%

SOURCE: IEA Third International Mathematics and Science Study (TIMSS), 1994-95.

Legend

☐ Percent of Students Internationally with Fully-Correct Response

■ Percent of Students Internationally with Partially-Correct Response

* Eighth grade in most countries; see Table 2 for information about the grades tested in each country.

• Percent correct reflects only the portion of the item score based on the quality of the data presentation; quality of data collection results are shown in Figure 3.4.

† One-point items; no partial-credit scores.

In Figure 3.5, profiles of international performance on example items in the mathematics performance expectation category of "Performing Mathematical Procedures" are presented for the eighth grade. Items requiring students to perform routine mathematical procedures (top panel) included performing calculations, completing a table, comparing frequencies, measuring, and performing conversions. Internationally, students did quite well on these types of items, with more than 65% of students providing fully-correct responses on all of the example items. Students had more difficulty, in general, on items requiring more complex mathematical procedures (bottom panel), such as drawing models to scale, identifying a pattern in numbers, drawing the net of a box, and constructing the net of a box to scale. There was much more variation in performance on items of this type, with performances ranging from 22% to 71% fully-correct responses.

Figure 3.6 shows international performance of eighth-grade students on example items in two subcategories of "Problem Solving and Mathematical Reasoning". Internationally, students demonstrated a range of performance on example items requiring them to predict, develop strategies, and solve problems (top panel). The highest percentage of fully-correct responses (73%) was on the routine application of a pattern, while only 11% of students received full credit for finding the correct factors of 455 in the Calculator task. There was also variation in performance on the three example items requiring students to generalize and conjecture (bottom panel).

The content area and context of the task seem to affect students' ability to express skills thought to be comparable regardless of the task (e.g., organizing and representing data shown in Figure 3.3). However, the overall familiarity of the task and its difficulty, as well as the nature of the cognitive processes required, also affect students' performance. For example, regardless of context, items requiring explanations were consistently more difficult than other types of questions. Similarly, less-familiar content like factoring

or circulation (Pulse task) also shows lower achievement across a variety of performance expectations. Generally, students were more successful in drawing conclusions from an experiment than in developing hypotheses about the causes of their findings, but the degree of the difference varied markedly in different countries. Large differences in performance were found between the use of more complex mathematical procedures like pattern identification or scaling, and familiar routine procedures, including the use of calculators (Figure 3.5). Internationally, the areas of greatest strength at the eighth grade were found in conducting investigations, executing more routine procedures, and solving problems, including some non-routine problems. Areas of greater difficulty were using more complex mathematical procedures and reasoning, as well as explaining and generalizing, both in science and mathematics. Fourth graders did well in conducting investigations in familiar content areas like electricity and magnetism, and they also did well in the use of procedural knowledge in science. In fact, the data show no difference internationally between fourth and eighth graders in the use of scientific procedures. For mathematics, however, use of procedures was sharply lower in fourth grade than in eighth grade in all countries.

Profiles of International Performance on Example Items That Require Performing Mathematical Procedures - Eighth Grade*

Figure 3.5

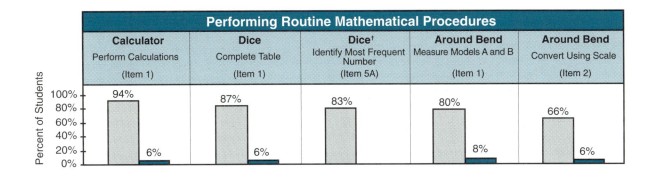

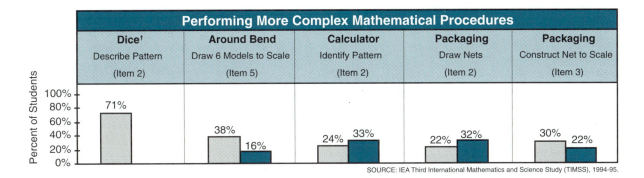

SOURCE: IEA Third International Mathematics and Science Study (TIMSS), 1994-95.

Legend

☐ Percent of Students Internationally with Fully-Correct Response

■ Percent of Students Internationally with Partially-Correct Response

* Eighth grade in most countries; see Table 2 for information about the grades tested in each country.

† One-point items; no partial credit scores.

| Figure 3.6 | Profiles of International Performance on Example Items That Require Problem Solving and Mathematical Reasoning - Eighth Grade* |

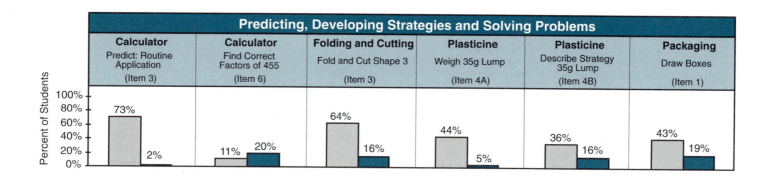

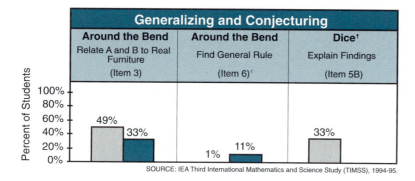

SOURCE: IEA Third International Mathematics and Science Study (TIMSS), 1994-95.

Legend

<svg>grey box</svg> Percent of Students Internationally with Fully-Correct Response

<svg>teal box</svg> Percent of Students Internationally with Partially-Correct Response

* Eighth grade in most countries; see Table 2 for information about the grades tested in each country.

† One-point items; no partial credit scores.

¹ Columbia did not administer this item; not included in international percentages.

Appendix

OVERVIEW OF TIMSS PROCEDURES FOR THE PERFORMANCE ASSESSMENT

HISTORY

TIMSS represents the continuation of a long series of studies conducted by the International Association for the Evaluation of Educational Achievement (IEA). Since its inception in 1959, the IEA has conducted more than 15 studies of cross-national achievement in curricular areas such as mathematics, science, language, civics, and reading. IEA conducted its First International Mathematics Study (FIMS) in 1964, and the Second International Mathematics Study (SIMS) in 1980-82. The First and Second International Science Studies (FISS and SISS) were conducted in 1970-71 and 1983-84, respectively. Since the subjects of mathematics and science are related in many respects and since there is broad interest in many countries in their students' abilities in both mathematics and science, the third studies were conducted together as an integrated effort.

The number of participating countries, the number of grades tested, and the assessment of mathematics and science simultaneously has resulted in TIMSS becoming the largest, most complex IEA study to date and the largest international study of educational achievement ever undertaken. Traditionally, IEA studies have systematically worked toward gaining more in-depth understanding of how various factors contribute to the overall outcomes of schooling. Particular emphasis has been given to refining our understanding of students' opportunity to learn as this opportunity becomes successively defined and implemented by curricular and instructional practices.

In an effort to extend what had been learned from previous studies and provide contextual and explanatory information, TIMSS expanded beyond the already substantial task of measuring achievement in two subject areas by also including a thorough investigation of curriculum and how it is delivered in classrooms around the world. In addition, extending the work of previous IEA studies, TIMSS included a performance assessment. In IEA's Second International Science Study a small subset of the participating countries administered practical tasks. TIMSS built on this experience and included more countries, more tasks, and a greater emphasis on an integration of conceptual knowledge and process skills. The inclusion of a performance assessment in TIMSS also reflected the current movement in education to measure students' understanding and competence with hands-on assessments.

THE COMPONENTS OF **TIMSS**

Continuing the approach of previous IEA studies, TIMSS addressed three conceptual levels of curriculum. The **intended curriculum** is composed of the mathematics and science instructional and learning goals as defined at the system level. The **implemented curriculum** is the mathematics and science curriculum as interpreted by teachers and made available to students. The **attained curriculum** is the mathematics and science content that students have learned and their attitudes towards these subjects. To aid in interpretation and comparison of results, TIMSS also collected extensive information about the social and cultural contexts for learning.

Nearly 50 countries participated in one or more of the various components of the TIMSS data collection effort, including the curriculum analysis. To gather information about the intended curriculum, mathematics and science specialists within each participating country worked section by section through curriculum guides, textbooks, and other curricular materials to categorize aspects of these materials in accordance with detailed specifications derived from the TIMSS mathematics and science curriculum frameworks.[1] Initial results from this component of TIMSS can be found in two companion volumes: *Many Visions, Many Aims: A Cross-National Investigation of Curricular Intentions in School Mathematics* and *Many Visions, Many Aims: A Cross-National Investigation of Curricular Intentions in School Science.*[2]

To measure the attained curriculum, TIMSS tested more than half a million students in mathematics and science at five grade levels. TIMSS included testing at three separate populations:

Population 1: Students enrolled in the two adjacent grades that contained the largest proportion of 9-year-old students at the time of testing – third- and fourth-grade students in most countries.

Population 2: Students enrolled in the two adjacent grades that contained the largest proportion of 13-year-old students at the time of testing – seventh- and eighth-grade students in most countries.

Population 3: Students in their final year of secondary education. As an additional option, countries could test two special subgroups of these students: students taking advanced courses in mathematics and students taking courses in physics.

Countries participating in the study were required to administer tests to the students in the two grades at Population 2 but could choose whether or not to participate at the other levels. Ten countries that participated in Population 1 and 21 countries that participated in Population 2 also administered the performance assessment to subsamples of the upper-grade students (eighth graders and fourth graders in most countries) who completed the written tests. Figure A.1 shows the countries that participated in the various components of TIMSS testing.

[1] Robitaille, D.F., McKnight, C.C., Schmidt, W.H., Britton, E.D., Raizen, S.A., and Nicol, C. (1993). *TIMSS Monograph No. 1: Curriculum Frameworks for Mathematics and Science*. Vancouver, B.C.: Pacific Educational Press.

[2] Schmidt, W.H., McKnight, C.C., Valverde, G.A., Houang, R.T., and Wiley, D.E. (1997). *Many Visions, Many Aims: A Cross-National Investigation of Curricular Intentions in School Mathematics*. Dordrecht, the Netherlands: Kluwer Academic Publishers.

Schmidt, W.H., Raizen, S.A., Britton, E.D., Bianchi, L.J., and Wolfe, R.G. (in press). *Many Visions, Many Aims: A Cross-National Investigation of Curricular Intentions in School Science*. Dordrecht, the Netherlands: Kluwer Academic Publishers.

TIMSS administered a broad array of questionnaires to collect data about how the curriculum is implemented in classrooms and about the social and cultural contexts for learning. Questionnaires were administered at the country level about decision-making and organizational features within the educational systems. The students who were tested answered questions pertaining to their attitudes towards mathematics and science, classroom activities, home background, and out-of-school activities. The mathematics and science teachers of sampled students responded to questions about teaching emphasis on the topics in the curriculum frameworks, instructional practices, textbook use, professional training and education, and their views on mathematics and science. The heads of schools responded to questions about school staffing and resources, mathematics and science course offerings, and support for teachers. In addition, a volume was compiled that presents descriptions of the educational systems of the participating countries.[3]

Achievement results and background data for Populations 1 and 2 (third, fourth, seventh, and eighth grades in many countries) have been published in four volumes.[4]

---

[3] Robitaille D.F. (Ed.). (1997). *National Contexts for Mathematics and Science Education: An Encyclopedia of Education Systems Participating in TIMSS.* Vancouver, B.C.: Pacific Educational Press.

[4] Mullis, I.V.S., Martin, M.O., Beaton, A.E., Gonzalez, E.J., Kelly, D.L., and Smith, T.A. (1997). *Mathematics Achievement in the Primary School Years: IEA's Third International Mathematics and Science Study.* Chestnut Hill, MA: Boston College.

Martin, M.O., Mullis, I.V.S., Beaton, A.E., Gonzalez, E.J., Smith, T.A., and Kelly, D.L. (1997). *Science Achievement in the Primary School Years: IEA's Third International Mathematics and Science Study.* Chestnut Hill, MA: Boston College

Beaton, A.E., Mullis, I.V.S., Martin, M.O. Gonzalez, E.J., Kelly, D.L., and Smith, T.A. (1996). *Mathematics Achievement in the Middle School Years: IEA's Third International Mathematics and Science Study.* Chestnut Hill, MA: Boston College.

Beaton, A.E., Martin, M.O., Mullis, I.V.S., Gonzalez, E.J., Smith, T.A., and Kelly, D.L. (1996). *Science Achievement in the Middle School Years: IEA's Third International Mathematics and Science Study.* Chestnut Hill, MA: Boston College.

Countries Participating in Components of TIMSS Testing | Figure A.1

Country	Population 1		Population 2		Population 3		
	Written Test	Performance Assessment	Written Test	Performance Assessment	Mathematics & Science Literacy	Advanced Mathematics	Physics
Argentina			●				
Australia	●	●	●	●	●	●	●
Austria	●		●		●	●	●
Belgium (Fl)			●				
Belgium (Fr)			●				
Bulgaria			●				
Canada	●	●	●	●	●	●	●
Colombia			●	●			
Cyprus	●	●	●	●	●	●	●
Czech Republic	●		●	●	●	●	●
Denmark			●		●	●	●
England	●		●	●			
France			●		●	●	●
Germany			●		●	●	●
Greece	●		●			●	
Hong Kong	●	●	●	●			
Hungary	●		●		●		
Iceland	●		●		●		
Indonesia	●		●				
Iran, Islamic Rep.	●	●	●	●			
Ireland	●		●				
Israel	●	●	●	●	●	●	●
Italy	●		●		●		
Japan	●		●				
Korea	●		●				
Kuwait	●		●				
Latvia	●		●				●
Lithuania			●		●	●	
Mexico	●		●		●	●	●
Netherlands	●		●	●	●		
New Zealand	●	●	●	●	●		
Norway	●		●	●	●		●
Philippines			●				
Portugal	●	●	●	●			
Romania			●	●			
Russian Federation			●		●	●	●
Scotland	●		●	●			
Singapore	●		●	●			
Slovak Republic			●				
Slovenia	●	●	●	●	●	●	●
South Africa			●		●		
Spain			●	●			
Sweden			●	●	●	●	●
Switzerland			●	●	●	●	●
Thailand	●	●	●				
United States	●	●	●	●	●	●	●

Developing the TIMSS Performance Assessment Tasks

The TIMSS performance assessment was developed by experts in mathematics, science, and performance assessment from participating countries. It was designed to reflect the TIMSS mathematics and science curriculum frameworks and be feasible for administration in a large-scale international assessment. In particular, attention was focused on developing tasks that represented the range of performance expectations in the TIMSS curriculum frameworks. The TIMSS Performance Assessment Committee developed a set of tasks, some of which were adapted from versions used in assessments in the United Kingdom, Australia, New Zealand, and the United States. In 1994, 22 tasks (at each population level) were field-tested in 19 countries. Based on the student results from this field test and evaluations of each task by field-test administrators, National Research Coordinators, and mathematics and science subject matter experts in the participating countries, 12 tasks for each population were selected for the performance assessment. Task selection was based on breadth of coverage, feasibility of obtaining materials and administering the tasks, time constraints, quality considerations noted by task reviewers, and field-test item statistics.[5] Difficulties in standardizing the use of live materials and soils, and differing climate effects – for example, great difficulty in keeping a moisture indicator dry in maritime climates – resulted in elimination of certain tasks, chiefly in the life and earth science areas, and reduced the overall content coverage to the physical sciences,

mathematics, and human biology. There were 13 tasks altogether; 11 were administered at both grades, although adaptations were made in the form of scaffolding for the younger age group, one unique task was administered to the fourth grade, and one unique task administered to the eighth grade. Table A.1 summarizes the mathematics and science content areas and the performance expectations associated with each of the performance assessment tasks.

The TIMSS performance assessment instruments were prepared in English and translated into the languages of administration. In addition, it sometimes was necessary to adapt the international versions for cultural purposes, even in the countries that tested in English. This process represented an enormous effort for the national centers, with many checks along the way. The translation effort included: 1) developing explicit guidelines for translation and cultural adaptation, 2) translation of the instruments by the national centers in accordance with the guidelines and by using two or more independent translators, 3) consultation with subject matter experts regarding cultural adaptations to ensure that the meaning and difficulty of items did not change, 4) verification of the quality of the translations by professional translators from an independent translation company, 5) correction by the national centers in accordance with the suggestions made, 6) verification that corrections were made, and 7) a series of statistical checks after the testing to detect items that did not perform comparably across countries.[6]

---

[5] See Chapter 1 of this report for a display of each task and student responses. Details of the criteria used for task selection are provided in Harmon, M. and Kelly, D.L. (1996). "Performance Assessment" in M.O. Martin and D.L. Kelly (Eds.), *Third International Mathematics and Science Study Technical Report, Volume I.* Chestnut Hill, MA: Boston College.

[6] More details about the translation verification procedures can be found in: Mullis, I.V.S., Kelly, D.L., and Haley, K. (1996). "Translation Verification Procedures" in M.O. Martin and I.V.S. Mullis (Eds.), *Third International Mathematics and Science Study: Quality Assurance in Data Collection.* Chestnut Hill, MA: Boston College. Maxwell, B. (1996). "Translation and Cultural Adaptation of the TIMSS Instruments" in M.O. Martin and D.L. Kelly (Eds.), *Third International Mathematics and Science Study Technical Report, Volume I.* Chestnut Hill, MA: Boston College.

Description of Performance Assessment Tasks with Associated Content Knowledge Areas and Performance Expectations (1 of 3)

Science Tasks

Task	Description	Content Areas		Performance Expectations
		Overall Task Content Areas	Specific Knowledge Areas	
Pulse	Student investigates changes in pulse rate during exercise; records and analyzes data; and explains results.	Life Science	• Life Process and Systems – Energy handling • Human Biology	• Conducting investigations • Gathering, organizing, and representing data • Interpreting investigational data • Applying scientific principles to develop explanations
Magnets	Student determines the stronger of two magnets and describes strategies to support conclusion.	Physical Science	• Energy and Physical Processes – Magnetism	• Conducting investigations • Interpreting investigational data • Formulating conclusions from investigational data
Batteries	Student determines which of four batteries are worn out; describes strategy; and uses concept knowledge to explain proper arrangement of batteries in a flashlight.	Physical Science	• Energy and Physical Processes – Electricity	• Conducting investigations • Interpreting investigational data • Formulating conclusions from investigational data • Applying scientific principles to solve problems and develop explanations
Rubber Band	Student investigates the effect on the length of a rubber band from attaching increasing numbers of masses; then explains results.	Physical Science	• Physical Properties of Matter – Elasticity	• Conducting investigations • Gathering, organizing, and representing data • Interpreting and extrapolating data • Applying scientific principles to develop explanations
Solutions	Student investigates the effect of different solvent temperatures on rate of solution; collects, records, and analyzes data; and explains results.	Physical Science	• Physical Properties of Matter – Solubility • Structure of Matter – Atoms, ions, molecules • Energy and Physical Processes – Heat and temperature • Physical Transformation – Dissolving – Explanations of physical changes	• Designing and conducting investigations • Using equipment • Gathering, organizing, and representing data • Formulating conclusions from investigational data • Applying scientific principles to develop explanations
Containers	Student investigates the effect of different container materials on heat transfer; draws a conclusion about the best insulator; and applies concept to a new, seemingly quite different problem.	Physical Science	• Physical Properties of Matter – Specific heat and temperature	• Conducting investigations • Using equipment • Gathering, organizing, and representing data • Formulating conclusions from investigational data • Applying scientific principles to develop explanations and solve new problems

SOURCE: IEA Third International Mathematics and Science Study (TIMSS), 1994-95.

Table A.1	Description of Performance Assessment Tasks with Associated Content Knowledge Areas and Performance Expectations (Continued – 2 of 3)

Combination Tasks

Task	Description	Content Areas		Performance Expectations
		Overall Task Content Areas	**Specific Knowledge Areas**	
Shadows	Student manipulates the positions of light source and object to find three positions where the shadow is twice the width of the object, and expresses the relationships of distances of the light and object to the screen as a general rule.	Physical Science	• Energy and Physical Processes – Light	**Science** • Conducting investigations • Gathering, organizing, and representing data • Interpreting investigational data • Formulating conclusions from investigational data • Applying scientific principles to develop explanations **Mathematics** • Performing routine and complex mathematical procedures • Problem solving • Conjecturing • Generalizing
		Mathematics	• Measurement and Units • Geometry: Position, Visualization, and Shape – Two-dimensional polygons • Geometry: Symmetry, Congruency and Similarity • Proportionality Problems	
Plasticine	Given only two standard masses, student develops and describes strategies to weigh lumps of various specified masses.	Physical Science	• Physical Properties of Matter – Weight and balance	**Science** • Conducting routine experimental procedures • Applying scientific principles to solve quantitative problems **Mathematics** • Performing routine mathematical procedures • Problem solving • Developing and describing strategy
		Mathematics	• Measurement and Units • Proportionality Concepts and Problems	

SOURCE: IEA Third International Mathematics and Science Study (TIMSS), 1994-95.

Description of Performance Assessment Tasks with Associated Content Knowledge Areas and Performance Expectations (Continued – 3 of 3)

Table A.1

Mathematics Tasks

Task	Description	Content Areas		Performance Expectations
		Overall Task Content Areas	**Specific Knowledge Areas**	
Dice	Student applies a given algorithm to numbers that are obtained from successive throws of a die, then explains why one resulting number occurs more frequently than others.	Mathematics	• Whole Number Operations • Data Representation and Analysis • Probability	• Performing routine and complex mathematical procedures • Conjecturing
Calculator	Student uses calculator for a series of multiplications, identifies pattern in the products, describes and extrapolates the pattern to solve a new problem. At eighth grade, student also draws on knowledge of number properties and factoring to find a set of factors.	Mathematics	• Whole Numbers: Meaning and Operations • Data Representation and Analysis	• Using equipment • Recalling mathematical objects and properties • Performing routine and complex mathematical procedures • Developing and describing strategy • Predicting
Folding and Cutting	Student reproduces patterns of increasing complexity by folding along axes of symmetry and cutting paper. At eighth grade, this is extended to drawing lines of symmetry without manipulating materials.	Mathematics	• Geometry: Symmetry Transformations	• Problem solving • Predicting

Around the Bend	Student uses models to determine which "furniture" will go around the bend in a corridor, uses scale to convert model dimensions (in centimeters) to real furniture dimensions (in meters), makes judgements about real-world applications, and develops a general rule.	Mathematics	• Measurement and Units
			• Geometry: Position, Visualization and Shape
			  – Two-dimensional polygons
			  – Three-dimensional
			• Proportionality Problems
				• Performing routine and complex mathematical procedures
				• Problem solving

Packaging	Student constructs boxes for three unique arrangements of four balls tightly packed; sketches nets for each box, and draws one net to actual size.	Mathematics	• Measurement and Units • Geometry: Position, Visualization and Shape – Three-dimensional	• Performing routine and complex mathematical procedures • Problem solving

SOURCE: IEA Third International Mathematics and Science Study (TIMSS), 1994-95.

PERFORMANCE ASSESSMENT DESIGN AND ADMINISTRATION PROCEDURES

The performance assessment was administered in a "circus" format in which the materials for 12 tasks (at each grade) were assembled at stations and students visited the stations according to one of two rotation plans to which they were assigned during the sampling process. In each administration, there were nine stations with materials for either one or two tasks. Students visited three stations, completing three to five tasks altogether. Each student spent 30 minutes at each station. The administration was designed to accommodate 9 students; at each school, either 9 or 18 students participated in the performance assessment.[7]

After completing the tasks at each station, students submitted their work booklets to the performance assessment administrator, together with any products. The work recorded in the booklets and any products created during the assessment were evaluated by coders specially trained to use the TIMSS scoring rubrics (see section on scoring the TIMSS performance assessment).

Each participating country was responsible for providing the materials for the performance assessment tasks and for administering the performance assessment, in accordance with the international procedures. The *Performance Assessment Administration Manual* specified the materials required for the tasks, the organization of tasks at stations in a "circus," assignment of students to stations, and all other aspects of the administration session. During the administration, the performance assessment administrator ensured that the students visited the correct stations and that supplies were replenished as necessary, and collected students' work. Several regional training sessions were conducted around the world during which representatives from the participating countries were trained in equipment set-up and administration procedures.

SAMPLE IMPLEMENTATION AND PARTICIPATION RATES

The selection of valid and efficient samples is crucial to the quality and success of an international comparative study such as TIMSS. The accuracy of the survey results depends on the quality of the available sampling information and on the quality of the sampling activities themselves. For TIMSS, National Research Coordinators (NRCs) worked on all phases of sampling with staff from Statistics Canada. NRCs received training in how to select the school and student samples and in the use of the sampling software. In consultation with the TIMSS sampling referee (Keith Rust, Westat, Inc.), staff from Statistics Canada reviewed the national sampling plans, sampling data, sampling frames, and sample execution. This documentation was used by the TIMSS International Study Center in consultation with Statistics Canada, the sampling referee, and the Technical Advisory Committee to evaluate the quality of the samples.

The sample of schools and students for the performance assessment was a subsample of the schools and students that participated in the main written assessment. Consequently, the characteristics of each country's performance assessment sample reflect the quality of the sampling for the written assessment and compliance with the guidelines for the performance assessment sampling.

In a few situations where it was not possible to implement TIMSS for all of Populations 1 and 2, as specified by the international desired population definition – all students in the upper grade of the two adjacent grades with the largest proportion of 9-year-olds (Population 1) and 13-year-olds (Population 2) – countries were permitted to define a national desired population that did not include part of the international desired population. Tables A.2 and A.3 show any differences in coverage between the international and national desired populations, at the upper grades of the target

---

[7] For more information on the performance assessment design see Harmon, M. and Kelly, D.L. (1996). "Performance Assessment" in M.O. Martin and D.L. Kelly (Eds.), *Third International Mathematics and Science Study Technical Report Volume I.* Chestnut Hill, MA: Boston College.

populations (eighth grade and fourth grade in most countries). Most participants achieved 100% coverage. The countries with less than 100% coverage are identified in the tables in this report. Israel defined its tested population according to the structure of its school system and tested only schools in the Hebrew education system. Switzerland administered TIMSS in the German-speaking cantons only.

For the main written assessment, within the desired population countries could define a population that excluded a small percentage (less than 10%) of certain kinds of schools or students that would be very difficult or resource-intensive to test (e.g., schools for students with special needs or schools that were very small or located in extremely remote areas). For the performance assessment, in the interest of ensuring the quality of the administration, countries could exclude additional schools if the schools had fewer than nine students in the upper grade and thus could not provide a full complement of students for the performance assessment rotation or if the schools were in a remote region. The exclusion rate for the performance assessment sample was not to exceed 25% of the national desired population. Tables A.2 and A.3 show the main assessment school exclusion rates, the performance assessment school exclusion rates, the within-sample exclusion rates, and the overall exclusion rates for the eighth and fourth grades, respectively. For various reasons, at the eighth grade England and Romania exceeded the 25% limit for performance assessment exclusions. At the fourth grade only New Zealand exceeded this limit. The exclusion rates for these countries are noted in the tables in this report.

For the main assessment, TIMSS used a two-stage sample design at Populations 1 and 2, where the first stage involved selecting 150 public and private schools within each country. Within each school,

countries were to use random procedures to select one fourth grade and one third grade mathematics class for Population 1 and one eighth grade and one seventh grade mathematics class at Population 2 (or the corresponding upper and lower grades in that country). All of the students in those two classes were to participate in the TIMSS testing. This approach was designed to yield a representative sample of approximately 7,500 students per country, with approximately 3,750 students at each grade.[8]

For the performance assessment, TIMSS participants were to sample at least 50 schools from those already selected for the written assessment, and from each school a sample of either 9 or 18 upper-grade students already selected for the written assessment. This yielded a sample of about 450 students in each of the eighth and fourth grades in each country. Typically, between 150 and 300 students in a country responded to each performance assessment task. Tables A.4 and A.5 show the school and student sample sizes for the main assessment sample and the performance assessment subsample for the eighth grade. Tables A.6 and A.7 show the corresponding information for the fourth grade.

Countries were required to obtain a participation rate of at least 85% of both schools and students, or a combined rate (the product of school and student participation) of 75%. Tables A.8 and A.9 present, for the eighth and fourth grades, respectively, the school, student, and overall participation rates for the main assessment and the performance assessment. Because the performance assessment sample is drawn from the main assessment sample, the participation rates achieved for the performance assessment reflect the participation of schools and students in the main assessment, as well as those for the performance assessment administration.

---

[8] The sample design for TIMSS is described in detail in Foy, P., Rust, K., and Schleicher, A. (1996). "TIMSS Sample Design" in M.O. Martin and D.L. Kelly (Eds.), *Third International Mathematics and Science Study, Technical Report, Volume I.* Chestnut Hill, MA: Boston College.

Table A.2 Coverage of TIMSS Target Population - Performance Assessment – Eighth Grade*

The international desired target population is defined as follows:
Eighth Grade - All students enrolled in the higher of the two adjacent grades with the largest proportion of 13-year-old students at the time of testing.

Country	International Desired Target Population		National Desired Target Population			
	Coverage	Notes	Main Assessment School-Level Exclusions	Performance Assessment School-Level Exclusions	Within-Sample Exclusions	Overall Exclusions
Australia	100%		0.2%	16.3%	0.6%	17.0%
Canada	100%		2.4%	15.0%	1.8%	19.1%
Colombia	100%		3.8%	0.0%	0.0%	3.8%
Cyprus	100%		0.0%	0.0%	0.0%	0.0%
Czech Republic	100%		4.9%	0.0%	0.0%	4.9%
[2] England	100%		8.4%	16.6%	2.4%	27.3%
Hong Kong	100%		2.0%	1.0%	0.0%	3.0%
Iran, Islamic Rep.	100%		0.3%	17.0%	0.0%	17.3%
[1] Israel	74%	Hebrew Public Education System	3.1%	0.0%	0.0%	3.1%
Netherlands	100%		1.2%	0.0%	0.0%	1.2%
New Zealand	100%		1.3%	10.5%	0.4%	12.1%
Norway	100%		0.3%	22.6%	1.5%	24.4%
Portugal	100%		0.0%	0.0%	0.3%	0.3%
[3] Romania	100%		2.8%	28.5%	0.0%	31.3%
Scotland	100%		0.3%	9.3%	1.7%	11.3%
Singapore	100%		4.6%	0.0%	0.0%	4.6%
Slovenia	100%		2.4%	0.7%	0.2%	3.2%
Spain	100%		6.0%	1.7%	2.6%	10.3%
Sweden	100%		0.0%	23.5%	0.7%	24.2%
[1] Switzerland	75%	German Cantons	4.4%	8.4%	0.8%	13.6%
United States	100%		0.4%	1.3%	1.7%	3.4%

SOURCE: IEA Third International Mathematics and Science Study (TIMSS), 1994-95.

* Eighth grade in most countries; see Table 2 for information about the grades tested in each country.

[1] National Desired Population does not cover all of International Desired Population.

[2] National Defined Population covers less than 90 percent of National Desired Population for the main assessment (school-level plust within-sample exclusions).

[3] School-level exclusions for performance assessment exceed 25% of the National Desired Population.

Because results are rounded to the nearest whole number, some totals may appear inconsistent.

Coverage of TIMSS Target Population - Performance Assessment – Fourth Grade* Table A.3

The international desired target population is defined as follows:
Fourth Grade - All students enrolled in the higher of the two adjacent grades with the largest proportion of 9-year-old students at the time of testing.

Country	International Desired Target Population		National Desired Target Population			
	Coverage	Notes	Main Assessment School-Level Exclusions	Performance Assessment School-Level Exclusions	Within-Sample Exclusions	Overall Exclusions
Australia	100%		0.1%	15.1%	1.4%	16.7%
Canada	100%		2.5%	15.4%	3.1%	21.0%
Cyprus	100%		3.1%	0.0%	0.1%	3.2%
Hong Kong	100%		2.6%	1.9%	0.0%	4.6%
Iran, Islamic Rep.	100%		0.3%	17.5%	0.9%	18.7%
[2] Israel	72%	Hebrew Public Education System	1.1%	0.0%	0.1%	1.2%
[1] New Zealand	100%		0.7%	25.8%	0.4%	27.0%
Portugal	100%		6.6%	0.0%	0.7%	7.3%
Slovenia	100%		1.9%	0.7%	0.0%	2.6%
United States	100%		0.4%	0.0%	4.3%	4.7%

SOURCE: IEA Third International Mathematics and Science Study (TIMSS), 1994-95.

* Fourth grade in most countries; see Table 2 for information about the grades tested in each country.
[1] School-level exclusions for performance assessment exceed 25% of the National Desired Population.
[2] National Desired Population does not cover all of International Desired Population.
Because results are rounded to the nearest whole number, some totals may appear inconsistent.

Table A.6 — TIMSS School Sample Sizes - Performance Assessment - Fourth Grade*

Country	Main Assessment					Performance Assessment				
	Number of Schools in Original Sample	Number of Eligible Schools in Original Sample	Number of Schools in Original Sample That Participated in Main Assessment	Number of Replacement Schools That Participated in Main Assessment	Total Number of Schools That Participated in Main Assessment	Number of Schools Eligible for Performance Assessment	Number of Schools Sampled for Performance Assessment	Number of Original Schools That Participated	Number of Replacement Schools That Participated	Total Number of Schools That Participated in Performance Assessment
Australia	268	268	169	9	178	122	50	41	5	46
Canada	423	420	390	0	390	319	84	75	1	76
Cyprus	150	150	146	0	146	150	50	49	1	50
Hong Kong	156	148	124	0	124	120	50	37	10	47
Iran, Islamic Rep.	180	180	180	0	180	140	50	49	1	50
Israel	100	100	40	0**	87	100	54	27	18	45
New Zealand	150	150	120	29	149	103	50	39	11	50
Portugal	150	150	143	0	143	150	50	48	0	48
Slovenia	150	150	121	0	121	149	50	49	1	50
United States	220	213	182	0	182	212	106	88	1	89

SOURCE: IEA Third International Mathematics and Science Study (TIMSS), 1994-95.

* Fourth grade in most countries; see Table 2 for information about the grades tested in each country.

**Does not include 47 replacement schools that were selected using unapproved methods.

TIMSS Student Sample Sizes - Performance Assessment – Fourth Grade* | Table A.7

| Country | Main Assessment | | | | | | Performance Assessment |
	Number of Sampled Students in Participating Schools	Number of Students Withdrawn from Class/School	Number of Students Excluded	Number of Students Eligible	Number of Students Absent	Total Number of Students Assessed	Total Number of Students Assessed
Australia	6930	37	104	6789	282	6507	513
Canada	9193	81	268	8844	436	8408	1150
Cyprus	3972	4	3	3965	589	3376	444
Hong Kong	4475	0	1	4474	63	4411	421
Iran, Islamic Rep.	3521	5	36	3480	95	3385	440
Israel	2486	0	3	2483	132	2351	402
New Zealand	2627	82	20	2525	104	2421	613
Portugal	2994	15	16	2963	110	2853	430
Slovenia	2720	3	0	2717	151	2566	447
United States	8224	61	412	7751	455	7296	777

SOURCE: IEA Third International Mathematics and Science Study (TIMSS), 1994-95.

* Fourth grade in most countries; see Table 2 for information about the grades tested in each country.

Table A.8 | TIMSS Participation Rates - Performance Assessment - Eighth Grade*

Country	Main Assessment					Performance Assessment				
	School Participation Rate Before Replacement (Weighted Percentage)	School Participation Rate After Replacement (Weighted Percentage)	Within-School Student Participation Rate (Weighted Percentage)	Overall Participation Rate Before Replacement (Weighted Percentage)	Overall Participation Rate After Replacement (Weighted Percentage)	School Participation Rate Before Replacement (Weighted Percentage)	School Participation Rate After Replacement (Weighted Percentage)	Within-School Student Participation Rate (Weighted Percentage)	Overall Participation Rate Before Replacement (Weighted Percentage)	Overall Participation Rate After Replacement (Weighted Percentage)
Australia	75%	77%	92%	69%	70%	51%	58%	73%	37%	43%
Canada	90%	91%	93%	84%	84%	97%	97%	92%	89%	89%
Colombia	91%	93%	94%	85%	87%	91%	91%	96%	88%	88%
Cyprus	100%	100%	97%	97%	97%	96%	96%	93%	88%	88%
Czech Republic	96%	100%	92%	89%	92%	94%	100%	82%	77%	82%
England	56%	85%	91%	51%	77%	46%	85%	84%	38%	71%
Hong Kong	82%	82%	98%	81%	81%	44%	44%	77%	34%	34%
Iran, Islamic Rep.	100%	100%	98%	98%	98%	98%	98%	93%	91%	91%
Israel	45%	46%	98%	44%	45%	44%**	46%**	30%**	13%**	14%**
Netherlands	24%	63%	95%	23%	60%	18%	48%	89%	16%	43%
New Zealand	91%	99%	94%	86%	94%	90%	100%	88%	79%	88%
Norway	91%	97%	96%	87%	93%	87%	96%	91%	79%	88%
Portugal	95%	95%	97%	92%	92%	96%	96%	91%	87%	87%
Romania	94%	94%	96%	89%	89%	90%	90%	94%	84%	84%
Scotland	79%	83%	88%	69%	73%	78%	96%	85%	66%	81%
Singapore	100%	100%	95%	95%	95%	90%	100%	87%	79%	87%
Slovenia	81%	81%	95%	77%	77%	98%	100%	93%	91%	93%
Spain	96%	100%	95%	91%	94%	94%	100%	93%	87%	93%
Sweden	97%	97%	93%	90%	90%	99%	99%	88%	87%	87%
Switzerland	93%	95%	98%	92%	94%	65%	81%	97%	63%	78%
United States	77%	85%	92%	71%	78%	71%	77%	86%	61%	66%

SOURCE: IEA Third International Mathematics and Science Study (TIMSS), 1994-95.

* Eighth grade in most countries; see Table 2 for information about the grades tested in each country.

**Unweighted participation rates.

TIMSS Participation Rates - Performance Assessment - Fourth Grade* Table A.9

Country	Main Assessment					Performance Assessment				
	School Participation Rate Before Replacement (Weighted Percentage)	School Participation Rate After Replacement (Weighted Percentage)	Within-School Student Participation Rate (Weighted Percentage)	Overall Participation Rate Before Replacement (Weighted Percentage)	Overall Participation Rate After Replacement (Weighted Percentage)	School Participation Rate Before Replacement (Weighted Percentage)	School Participation Rate After Replacement (Weighted Percentage)	Within-School Student Participation Rate (Weighted Percentage)	Overall Participation Rate Before Replacement (Weighted Percentage)	Overall Participation Rate After Replacement (Weighted Percentage)
Australia	66%	69%	96%	63%	66%	47%	56%	76%	36%	43%
Canada	90%	90%	96%	86%	86%	91%	92%	95%	87%	88%
Cyprus	97%	97%	86%	83%	83%	98%	100%	86%	85%	86%
Hong Kong	84%	84%	98%	83%	83%	61%	77%	95%	58%	73%
Iran, Islamic Rep.	100%	100%	97%	97%	97%	97%	100%	93%	90%	93%
Israel	40%	40%	94%	38%	38%	50% **	83% **	30% **	15% **	25% **
New Zealand	80%	99%	96%	77%	95%	72%	93%	90%	65%	83%
Portugal	95%	95%	96%	92%	92%	96%	96%	94%	91%	91%
Slovenia	81%	81%	94%	76%	76%	98%	100%	91%	89%	91%
United States	85%	85%	94%	80%	80%	83%	84%	88%	73%	74%

SOURCE: IEA Third International Mathematics and Science Study (TIMSS), 1994-95.

* Fourth grade in most countries; see Table 2 for information about the grades tested in each country.
**Unweighted participation rates.

COMPLIANCE WITH SAMPLING GUIDELINES

Figure A.2 shows how countries have been grouped in tables in this report. Countries that complied with the TIMSS guidelines for grade selection and classroom sampling, and that achieved acceptable participation rates – 85% of both the schools and students or a combined rate (the product of school and student participation) of 75% with or without replacement schools, are shown in the first panel of Figure A.2. These countries (12 at the eighth grade and 5 at the fourth grade) appear in the tables in this report ordered by achievement. Countries that met the guidelines only after including replacement schools are so labeled.

Countries that did not reach at least 50% school participation without the use of replacement schools, or that failed to reach the sampling participation standard even with the inclusion of replacement schools, are shown in the second panel of Figure A.2. These countries are presented in a separate section of the tables presenting task performance.

To provide a better curricular match, for the written assessment at Population 2, Colombia, Romania, and Slovenia elected to test their seventh- and eighth-grade students, even though that meant not testing the two grades with the most 13-year-olds. Their students were thus somewhat older than those in the other countries. As a result, the students sampled for the performance assessment (eighth graders) also are somewhat older than those in other countries. At Population 1, Slovenia tested their third- and fourth-grade students for the written assessment even though these were not the two grades with the most 9-year-olds. Consequently, their fourth graders who were sampled for the performance assessment are somewhat older than students in other countries. Colombia and Romania did not participate in TIMSS at the primary grades. See Table A.10 for the percentages of 9- and 13-year-olds in the target grades. In this report, Colombia, Romania, and Slovenia are presented in alphabetical order in a separate section of the tables presenting task results.

At the eighth grade, Hong Kong's sample size for the performance assessment was very small due to low school participation, and thus its eighth-grade results are presented in Appendix B. Israel did not completely comply with the TIMSS within-school sampling procedures at the eighth and fourth grades and it had a small sample size at the eighth grade; its results are also presented in Appendix B.

Countries Grouped for Reporting of Performance Assessment Results According to Their Compliance with Guidelines for Sample Implementation and Participation Rates

Figure A.2

Eighth Grade	Fourth Grade
Countries satisfying guidelines for sample participation rates, grade selection and sampling procedures	
Canada Cyprus Czech Republic Iran, Islamic Republic New Zealand Norway Portugal [†] Scotland Singapore Spain Sweden [††] Switzerland	Canada Cyprus Iran, Islamic Republic [†3] New Zealand Portugal
Countries not satisfying guidelines for sample participation rates	
Australia [2] England Netherlands United States	Australia Hong Kong United States
Countries not meeting age/grade specifications (high percentage of older students)	
Colombia [3] Romania Slovenia	Slovenia
Countries with small sample sizes	
Hong Kong	
Countries with unapproved sampling procedures	
[4] Israel	Israel

SOURCE: IEA Third International Mathematics and Science Study (TIMSS), 1994-95.

[†] Met guidelines for sample participation rates only after replacement schools were included.

[1] National Desired Population does not cover all of International Desired Population (see Table A.2) - German-speaking cantons only.

[2] National Defined Population covers less than 90 percent of National Desired Population for the main assessment (see Table A.2).

[3] School-level exclusions for performance assessment exceed 25% of the National Desired Population (see Tables A.2 and A.3).

[4] Israel also had a small size at the eighth grade.

Table A.10   Coverage of 13-Year Old and 9-Year-Old Students

Country	13-Year-Old Students			9-Year-Old-Students		
	Percent in Lower Grade (Seventh Grade*)	Percent in Upper Grade (Eighth Grade*)	Percent in Both Grades	Percent in Lower Grade (Third Grade*)	Percent in Upper Grade (Fourth Grade*)	Percent in Both Grades
Australia	64	28	92	65	29	94
Canada	48	43	91	46	48	94
Colombia	30	15	45	.	.	.
Cyprus	28	70	98	35	63	98
Czech Republic	73	17	90	.	.	.
England	57	42	99	.	.	.
Hong Kong	44	46	90	43	50	93
Iran, Islamic Rep.	47	25	72	51	32	83
Israel	-	-	-	-	-	-
Netherlands	59	31	90	.	.	.
New Zealand	52	47	99	50	49	99
Norway	43	57	100	.	.	.
Portugal	44	32	76	45	48	93
Romania	67	9	76	.	.	.
Scotland	24	75	99	.	.	.
Singapore	82	15	97	.	.	.
Slovenia	65	2	67	60	0	60
Spain	46	39	85	.	.	.
Sweden	45	54	99	.	.	.
Switzerland	48	44	92	.	.	.
United States	58	33	91	61	34	95

SOURCE: IEA Third International Mathematics and Science Study (TIMSS), 1994-95.

* Seventh, eighth, third, and fourth grades in most countries; see Table 2 for information about the upper grades tested in each country. The international definition is the two adjacent grades with the largest proportion of 13-year-old students, and the two with the largest proportion of 9-year-old students.

A dash (-) indicates data are not available. Israel did not test the lower grades.

A dot (.) indicates country did not participate in performance assessment at the fourth grade.

SCORING THE PERFORMANCE ASSESSMENT

TIMSS developed detailed scoring rubrics in order to obtain the maximum amount of information from the constructed responses and to evaluate students' work reliably. The scoring system for the performance assessment used the same type of two-digit codes as the free-response items of the written test.[9] The first digit designates the correctness level of the response (3, 2, 1, or 0 points). The second digit, combined with the first, represents a diagnostic code used to identify specific types of approaches, strategies, or common errors and misconceptions. Although not used in this report, analyses of responses based on the complete two-digit code should provide insight into ways to help students better understand science and mathematics concepts and problem-solving approaches.

To meet the goal of implementing reliable scoring procedures based on the TIMSS rubrics, the TIMSS International Study Center prepared guides containing the rubrics and explanations of how to apply them, together with example student responses for the various rubric categories. These guides, together with additional practice responses, were used as a basis for a series of regional training sessions. These were designed to assist representatives of national centers who would then be responsible for training personnel in their respective countries to apply the two-digit codes reliably.[10]

To gather and document empirical information about the within-country agreement among scorers, TIMSS developed a procedure whereby systematic subsamples of approximately 10% of the students' responses in each country were to be coded independently by two different scorers. Tables A.11 and A.12 display the intercoder agreement for the eighth and fourth grades, respectively. Data are presented for 12 countries at the eighth grade and for 4 countries at the fourth grade. Unfortunately, lack of resources prevented several countries from providing this information. The range and average across all performance assessment items of percent exact agreement are reported for both the correctness score and the full two-digit diagnostic code. A high percentage of exact agreement was observed for most items, especially at the correctness score level. At the eighth grade, the average percent exact agreement across items for the correctness score ranged from 79% to 100% across countries, with an overall average for all 12 countries of 91%. At the fourth grade, the country-level averages ranged from 91% to 99%, with an overall average of 93%. It should be noted that due to the smaller sample sizes in the performance assessment, in some countries only a small number of student responses for each item were available in the reliability sample.

---

[9] For more information on the TIMSS scoring procedures, see Lie, S., Taylor, A., and Harmon, M. (1996). "Scoring Techniques and Criteria" in M.O. Martin and D.L. Kelly (Eds.), *Third International Mathematics and Science Study Technical Report, Volume I.* Chestnut Hill, MA: Boston College.

[10] The procedures used in the training sessions are documented in Mullis, I.V.S., Garden, R.A., and Jones, C.A. (1996). "Training for Scoring the TIMSS Free-Response Items" in M.O. Martin and D.L. Kelly (Eds.), *Third International Mathematics and Science Study Technical Report, Volume I.* Chestnut Hill, MA: Boston College.

Table A.11 TIMSS Inter-Coder Agreement for Performance Assessment – Eighth Grade*

Country	Correctness Score Agreement			Diagnostic Code Agreement			Average Number of Student Responses per Item in the Reliability Sample▼
	Average Percent of Exact Agreement Across Tasks	Range of Percent of Exact Agreement		Average Percent of Exact Agreement Across Tasks	Range of Percent of Exact Agreement		
		Min	Max		Min	Max	
Australia	92	63	100	83	43	100	30
Colombia	94	68	100	82	40	100	18
Czech Republic	96	78	100	91	70	100	27
Hong Kong	89	56	100	80	44	100	9
Netherlands	82	52	100	71	22	100	23
Norway	88	67	100	81	40	100	15
Portugal	100	91	100	96	73	100	12
Scotland	79	46	100	70	27	100	12
Singapore	97	76	100	94	68	100	25
Spain	93	68	100	88	52	100	24
Switzerland	96	77	100	92	77	100	24
United States	85	62	100	74	46	100	59
AVERAGE	91	67	100	84	50	100	23

SOURCE: IEA Third International Mathematics and Science Study (TIMSS), 1994-95.

* Eighth grade in most countries; see Table 2 for information about the grades tested in each country.

▼ Number of student responses per item in reliability sample averaged over all items.

Note: Reliablity data based on 64 scored item parts. Percent agreement was computed separately for each part, and each part was treated as a separate item in computing averages and ranges. Reliability data are not available for one item (Magnets, Item 2).

Reliability data are not available for the following countries: Canada, Cyprus, England, Iran, Israel, New Zealand, Romania, Slovenia, and Sweden.

Because results are rounded to the nearest whole number, some totals may appear inconsistent.

TIMSS Inter-Coder Agreement for Performance Assessment – Fourth Grade*   Table A.12

Country	Correctness Score Agreement			Diagnostic Code Agreement			Average Number of Student Responses per Item in the Reliability Sample▼
	Average Percent of Exact Agreement Across Tasks	Range of Percent of Exact Agreement		Average Percent of Exact Agreement Across Tasks	Range of Percent of Exact Agreement		
		Min	Max		Min	Max	
Australia	91	69	100	80	41	100	30
Hong Kong	93	75	100	86	56	100	16
Portugal	99	89	100	97	83	100	18
United States	89	60	100	77	41	100	67
AVERAGE	93	73	100	85	56	100	33

SOURCE: IEA Third International Mathematics and Science Study (TIMSS), 1994-95.

* Fourth grade in most countries; see Table 2 for information about the grades tested in each country.

▼ Number of student responses per item in reliability sample averaged over all items.

Note: Reliablity data based on 56 scored item parts. Percent agreement was computed separately for each part, and each part was treated as a separate item in computing averages and ranges. Reliability data are not available for one item (Magnets, Item 2).

Reliability data are not available for the following countries: Canada, Cyprus, Iran, Israel, New Zealand, Slovenia.

Because results are rounded to the nearest whole number, some totals may appear inconsistent.

PERFORMANCE ASSESSMENT TEST RELIABILITY

Table A.13 displays a measure of the reliability of the performance assessment test as a whole for each country for the eighth and fourth grades. This coefficient is the KR-21 reliability coefficient across the items in all tasks computed from the correlation matrix based on all available data for each country. Reliabilities for the fourth grade ranged from .85 to .89 and in the eighth grade from .86 to .94. The international median, shown in the last row of the table, is the median of the reliability coefficients for all countries. These international medians are .88 for the fourth grade and .90 for the eighth grade.

DATA PROCESSING

To ensure the availability of comparable, high-quality data for analysis, TIMSS carried out a set of rigorous quality control steps to create the international database.[11] TIMSS prepared manuals and software for countries to use in entering their data so that the information would be in a standardized international format before being forwarded to the IEA Data Processing Center in Hamburg for creation of the international database. Upon arrival at the IEA Data Processing Center, the data from each country underwent an exhaustive cleaning process. The data cleaning process involved several iterative steps and procedures designed to identify, document, and correct deviations from the international instruments, file structures, and coding schemes. This process also emphasized consistency of information within national data sets and appropriate linking among the many student, teacher, and school data files.

Throughout the process, the data were checked and double-checked by the IEA Data Processing Center, the TIMSS International Study Center, and the national centers. The national centers were contacted regularly and given multiple opportunities to review the data for their countries. In conjunction with the Australian Council for Educational Research (ACER), the TIMSS International Study Center reviewed item statistics for each performance assessment item in each country to identify poorly performing items. Usually the poor statistics were a result of translation, adaptation, or printing deviations.

---

[11] These steps are detailed in Jungclaus, H. and Bruneforth, M. (1996). "Data Consistency Checking Across Countries" in M.O. Martin and D.L. Kelly, (Eds.), *Third International Mathematics and Science Study Technical Report, Volume I.* Chestnut Hill, MA: Boston College.

Reliability Coefficients[1] for the TIMSS Performance Assessment Eighth and Fourth Grades*

Table A.13

Country	Eighth Grade	Fourth Grade
Australia	0.90	0.87
Canada	0.89	0.85
Colombia	0.89	.
Cyprus	0.92	0.88
Czech Republic	0.93	.
England	0.93	.
Hong Kong	-	0.87
Iran, Islamic Rep.	0.89	0.89
Israel	-	-
Netherlands	0.88	.
New Zealand	0.90	0.85
Norway	0.89	.
Portugal	0.89	0.88
Romania	0.89	.
Scotland	0.94	.
Singapore	0.91	.
Slovenia	0.86	0.88
Spain	0.89	.
Sweden	0.92	.
Switzerland	0.90	.
United States	0.92	0.88
International Median	0.90	0.88

SOURCE: IEA Third International Mathematics and Science Study (TIMSS), 1994-95.

* Eighth and fourth grades in most countries; see Table 2 for information about the grades tested in each country.

[1] The reliability coefficient for each country is the KR-21 reliability coefficient across the tasks computed from the correlation matrix based on all available data for the country.

A dash (-) indicates data are not available.

A dot (.) indicates country did not participate at the fourth grade.

DATA ANALYSIS

The analytic approach underlying the majority of the results presented in this report involved calculating the average percentage score on each item within each task. The percentage score on an item is the score achieved by a student expressed as a percentage of the maximum points available on that item. The average percentage score shown for each item in Chapter 1 is this score averaged over the students in each country.

The overall task averages for each country shown in Chapter 1 (also shown in Tables 2.1 and 2.2) were obtained by averaging that country's average percentage scores across all items in a task, with each item being weighted equally. The unweighted average of items within a task was chosen to equalize the contribution of each item, since the scoring scheme for each item was developed independently, and the maximum point values were not required to be comparable across items. The overall averages for each country shown in Chapter 2 (also shown in Tables 3.1 to 3.4) reflect that country's task-level average percentage scores averaged across all tasks, with each task weighted equally. The international averages shown in all tables in Chapters 1 and 2 are the unweighted averages of the country-level average percentage scores.

Two different methods of analysis were used for the results shown in Chapter 3 on performance expectations. The average percentage scores by performance expectation categories in Tables 3.1 to 3.4 were computed by the method described in the previous paragraph. In these tables, however, average percentage scores for subsets of items were computed based on their assignment to performance expectation categories. The average of percentage scores across all tasks (shown in the first column) are the same as the overall averages computed in Chapter 2. Again, the international averages reflect the unweighted average of the country-level average percentage scores for each category.

Results shown in Figures 3.2 to 3.6 are based on calculating the percentage of students internationally obtaining full credit (maximum points) and also the percentage obtaining partial credit (one point on a two-point item; one or two points on a three-point item) on each example item.

ESTIMATING SAMPLING ERROR

Because the statistics presented in this report are estimates of national performance based on samples of students, rather than the values that could be calculated if every student in every country had answered every question, it is important to have measures of the degree of uncertainty of the estimates. The jackknife procedure was used to estimate the standard error associated with each statistic presented in this report. The use of confidence intervals, based on the standard errors, provides a way to make inferences about the population means and proportions in a manner that reflects the uncertainty associated with the sample estimates. An estimated sample statistic plus or minus two standard errors represents a 95% confidence interval for the corresponding population result.

Appendix B

SELECTED PERFORMANCE ASSESSMENT RESULTS FOR HONG KONG AND ISRAEL

Table B.1 — Hong Kong: Average Percentage Scores on Items by Task* - Eighth Grade

Pulse Task

Overall Task Average▼	Item 1 Measure Pulse		Item 2 Describe Trend	Item 3 Explain Results
	Presentation	Data Quality		
54 (3.3)	55 (6.0)	51 (5.7)	76 (4.1)	34 (3.8)

Magnet Task

Overall Task Average▼	Item 1 Identify Magnet	Item 2 Describe Strategy
88 (3.5)	94 (2.7)	82 (5.1)

Batteries Task

Overall Task Average▼	Item 1 Identify Good/Bad Batteries	Item 2 Describe Tests	Item 3 Identify Arrangement	Item 4 Explain Arrangement
64 (3.2)	75 (4.0)	51 (6.5)	96 (2.4)	34 (5.5)

Rubber Band Task

Overall Task Average▼	Item 1 Measure Lengths		Item 2 Graph Results	Item 3 Calculate Increase	Item 4 Describe Trend	Item 5 Predict Length	Item 6 Explain Prediction
	Presentation	Data Quality					
63 (3.2)	76 (4.6)	88 (4.5)	63 (4.5)	55 (5.3)	59 (3.0)	51 (5.3)	48 (5.5)

Solutions Task

Overall Task Average▼	Item 1 Plan Investigation	Item 2 Conduct Investigation		Item 3 Draw Conclusions	Item 4 Explain Conclusion	Item 5 Evaluate Design
		Presentation	Data Quality			
36 (3.4)	16 (3.6)	48 (5.9)	51 (6.1)	71 (6.2)	20 (3.7)	12 (4.4)

Shadows Task

Overall Task Average▼	Item 1 Describe Observation	Item 2 Explain Observation	Item 3 Problem Solve and Record Distances	Item 4 Describe Investigation	Item 5 Present Measurements	Item 6 Conclude and Generalize
27 (2.2)	56 (4.2)	35 (3.8)	27 (4.0)	23 (3.4)	12 (2.9)	10 (3.7)

SOURCE: IEA Third International Mathematics and Science Study (TIMSS), 1994-95.

* Percent of total possible points on each item averaged over students.

▼Average of percentage scores across items; all items weighted equally.

() Standard errors appear in parentheses. Because results are rounded to the nearest whole number, some totals may appear inconsistent.

Plasticine Task

Overall Task Average▼	Item 1A Weigh 20g Lump	Item 1B Describe Strategy 20g Lump	Item 2A Weigh 10g Lump	Item 2B Describe Strategy 10g Lump	Item 3A Weigh 15g Lump	Item 3B Describe Strategy 15g Lump	Item 4A Weigh 35g Lump	Item 4B Describe Strategy 35g Lump
52 (3.7)	92 (2.9)	80 (4.8)	56 (6.0)	55 (5.5)	44 (5.8)	28 (7.9)	27 (5.2)	36 (6.1)

Dice Task

Overall Task Average▼	Item 1 Complete Table	Item 2 Describe Pattern	Item 3 Apply Algorithm	Item 4 Count Frequencies	Item 5A Identify Most Frequent Number	Item 5B Explain Findings
77 (2.4)	93 (2.2)	73 (7.4)	94 (2.6)	70 (4.0)	84 (3.9)	48 (6.7)

Calculator Task

Overall Task Average▼	Item 1 Perform Calculations	Item 2 Identify Pattern	Item 3 Predict: Routine Application	Item 4 Predict: Non-Routine Application	Item 5 Explain Predictions	Item 6 Factors of 455 Reasons Factors Incorrect	Item 6 Factors of 455 Find Correct Factors
55 (1.9)	98 (1.0)	38 (6.3)	90 (2.6)	65 (4.0)	35 (4.8)	37 (2.4)	19 (4.2)

Folding and Cutting Task

Overall Task Average▼	Item 1 Fold and Cut Shape 1	Item 2 Fold and Cut Shape 2	Item 3 Fold and Cut Shape 3	Item 4 Predict and Draw Shape 4
76 (4.8)	77 (5.2)	80 (4.7)	78 (5.2)	70 (6.3)

Around the Bend Task

Overall Task Average▼	Item 1 Measure Models A and B	Item 2 Convert Using Scale	Item 3 Relate A and B to Real Furniture	Item 4 Solve Problem With A and B	Item 5 Six Models — Draw Models to Scale	Item 5 Six Models — Relate Models to Real Furniture	Item 5 Six Models — Solve Problem with Models	Item 6 Find General Rule
56 (2.5)	87 (3.7)	72 (4.6)	61 (4.0)	71 (5.3)	46 (6.1)	42 (4.5)	60 (4.3)	9 (3.2)

Packaging Task

Overall Task Average▼	Item 1 Draw Boxes	Item 2 Draw Nets	Item 3 Construct Net to Scale
54 (3.4)	53 (5.0)	55 (5.1)	53 (4.5)

SOURCE: IEA Third International Mathematics and Science Study (TIMSS), 1994-95.

* Percent of total possible points on each item averaged over students.

▼Average of percentage scores across items; all items weighted equally.

() Standard errors appear in parentheses. Because results are rounded to the nearest whole number, some totals may appear inconsistent.

Table B.2 Israel: Average Percentage Scores on Items by Task* - Unweighted Data Eighth Grade

Pulse Task

Overall Task Average▼	Item 1 Measure Pulse		Item 2 Describe Trend	Item 3 Explain Results
	Presentation	Data Quality		
62 (2.9)	67 (5.7)	43 (4.5)	84 (3.2)	55 (5.0)

Magnet Task

Overall Task Average▼	Item 1 Identify Magnet	Item 2 Describe Strategy
88 (3.6)	77 (6.5)	98 (1.9)

Batteries Task

Overall Task Average▼	Item 1 Identify Good/Bad Batteries	Item 2 Describe Tests	Item 3 Identify Arrangement	Item 4 Explain Arrangement
65 (4.2)	52 (10.1)	55 (7.3)	98 (1.8)	54 (3.3)

Rubber Band Task

Overall Task Average▼	Item 1 Measure Lengths		Item 2 Graph Results	Item 3 Calculate Increase	Item 4 Describe Trend	Item 5 Predict Length	Item 6 Explain Prediction
	Presentation	Data Quality					
75 (2.7)	91 (3.2)	93 (2.7)	65 (9.2)	60 (6.4)	61 (3.7)	85 (5.5)	69 (3.9)

Solutions Task

Overall Task Average▼	Item 1 Plan Investigation	Item 2 Conduct Investigation		Item 3 Draw Conclusions	Item 4 Explain Conclusion	Item 5 Evaluate Design
		Presentation	Data Quality			
64 (1.3)	56 (4.5)	77 (5.2)	61 (6.0)	91 (4.2)	57 (5.8)	40 (6.1)

Shadows Task

Overall Task Average▼	Item 1 Describe Observation	Item 2 Explain Observation	Item 3 Problem Solve and Record Distances	Item 4 Describe Investigation	Item 5 Present Measurements	Item 6 Conclude and Generalize
43 (3.8)	92 (2.8)	29 (6.0)	25 (3.3)	46 (7.8)	48 (8.4)	18 (5.3)

SOURCE: IEA Third International Mathematics and Science Study (TIMSS), 1994-95.

* Percent of total possible points on each item averaged over students.

▼Average of percentage scores across items; all items weighted equally.

() Standard errors appear in parentheses. Because results are rounded to the nearest whole number, some totals may appear inconsistent.

Israel: Average Percentage Scores on Items by Task* - Unweighted Data Eighth Grade (Continued)

Plasticine Task

Overall Task Average▼	Item 1A Weigh 20g Lump	Item 1B Describe Strategy 20g Lump	Item 2A Weigh 10g Lump	Item 2B Describe Strategy 10g Lump	Item 3A Weigh 15g Lump	Item 3B Describe Strategy 15g Lump	Item 4A Weigh 35g Lump	Item 4B Describe Strategy 35g Lump
78 (4.6)	98 (2.0)	91 (5.9)	96 (4.1)	61 (10.0)	91 (5.0)	51 (8.8)	79 (8.6)	53 (9.3)

Dice Task

Overall Task Average▼	Item 1 Complete Table	Item 2 Describe Pattern	Item 3 Apply Algorithm	Item 4 Count Frequencies	Item 5A Identify Most Frequent Number	Item 5B Explain Findings
74 (3.1)	87 (5.0)	58 (6.0)	91 (4.1)	71 (5.9)	80 (2.8)	56 (6.4)

Calculator Task

Overall Task Average▼	Item 1 Perform Calculations	Item 2 Identify Pattern	Item 3 Predict: Routine Application	Item 4 Predict: Non-Routine Application	Item 5 Explain Predictions	Item 6 Factors of 455 — Reasons Factors Incorrect	Item 6 Factors of 455 — Find Correct Factors
63 (2.3)	98 (1.1)	46 (6.9)	83 (5.4)	64 (4.8)	41 (6.4)	67 (2.1)	39 (4.6)

Folding and Cutting Task

Overall Task Average▼	Item 1 Fold and Cut Shape 1	Item 2 Fold and Cut Shape 2	Item 3 Fold and Cut Shape 3	Item 4 Predict and Draw Shape 4
67 (5.5)	70 (6.2)	72 (6.6)	69 (5.1)	57 (5.8)

Around the Bend Task

Overall Task Average▼	Item 1 Measure Models A and B	Item 2 Convert Using Scale	Item 3 Relate A and B to Real Furniture	Item 4 Solve Problem With A and B	Item 5 Six Models — Draw Models to Scale	Item 5 Six Models — Relate Models to Real Furniture	Item 5 Six Models — Solve Problem with Models	Item 6 Find General Rule
62 (2.1)	83 (5.3)	74 (7.6)	79 (4.0)	69 (5.8)	48 (6.9)	67 (4.7)	60 (3.9)	14 (4.8)

Packaging Task

Overall Task Average▼	Item 1 Draw Boxes	Item 2 Draw Nets	Item 3 Construct Net to Scale
58 (5.4)	55 (5.4)	63 (6.6)	56 (9.1)

SOURCE: IEA Third International Mathematics and Science Study (TIMSS), 1994-95.

* Percent of total possible points on each item averaged over students.

▼Average of percentage scores across items; all items weighted equally.

() Standard errors appear in parentheses. Because results are rounded to the nearest whole number, some totals may appear inconsistent.

Table B.3 — Israel: Average Percentage Scores on Items by Task* - Unweighted Data Fourth Grade

Pulse Task

Overall Task Average▼	Item 1 Measure Pulse at Rest	Item 2 Measure Pulse During Exercise	Item 3 Describe Trend	Item 4 Explain Results
54 (2.5)	72 (5.0)	64 (3.7)	57 (4.1)	22 (2.0)

Magnet Task

Overall Task Average▼	Item 1 Identify Stronger Magnet	Item 2 Describe Strategy
93 (1.8)	93 (2.5)	94 (2.0)

Batteries Task

Overall Task Average▼	Item 1 Identify Good/Bad Batteries	Item 2 Describe Tests	Item 3 Identify Arrangement	Item 4 Explain Arrangement
46 (2.3)	39 (4.3)	23 (3.1)	82 (3.8)	39 (2.3)

Rubber Band Task

Overall Task Average▼	Item 1 Record Lengths	Item 2 Calculate Increase	Item 3 Describe Trend	Item 4 Predict Length	Item 5 Explain Prediction
61 (1.5)	95 (1.1)	48 (3.6)	57 (2.7)	62 (3.6)	43 (3.6)

Containers Task

Overall Task Average▼	Item 1 Measure Temperatures and Record in Table		Item 2 Identify Best Insulator	Item 3 Explain Best Insulator	Item 4 Apply to Ice Cream	Item 5 Explain Application
	Ability to Use Thermometer	Quality of Data Gathering				
40 (1.7)	87 (3.8)	72 (4.3)	39 (3.1)	11 (2.3)	23 (3.3)	5 (1.6)

Shadows Task

Overall Task Average▼	Item 1 Describe Shadow: Closer	Item 2 Describe Shadow: Further	Item 3 Measure Shadow Width	Item 4 Measure Distance	Item 5 Record 3 More Measurements	Item 6 Explain Shadow Size	Item 7 Find General Rule
35 (1.9)	74 (3.6)	77 (3.7)	26 (3.4)	27 (5.0)	20 (2.3)	12 (2.6)	7 (2.5)

SOURCE: IEA Third International Mathematics and Science Study (TIMSS), 1994-95.

* Percent of total possible points on each item averaged over students.

▼Average of percentage scores across items; all items weighted equally.

() Standard errors appear in parentheses. Because results are rounded to the nearest whole number, some totals may appear inconsistent.

Plasticine Task

Overall Task Average▼	Item 1A Weigh 20g Lump	Item 1B Describe Strategy 20g Lump	Item 2A Weigh 10g Lump	Item 2B Describe Strategy 10g Lump	Item 3A Weigh 30g Lump	Item 3B Describe Strategy 30g Lump	Item 4A Weigh 15g Lump	Item 4B Describe Strategy 15g Lump
56 (3.8)	75 (5.8)	74 (4.2)	59 (6.4)	39 (3.8)	68 (6.1)	53 (5.3)	54 (4.8)	30 (4.7)

Dice Task

Overall Task Average▼	Item 1 Complete Table	Item 2 Describe Pattern	Item 3 Apply Algorithm	Item 4 Count Frequencies	Item 5A Identify Most Frequent Number	Item 5B Explain Findings
58 (2.4)	73 (3.3)	48 (3.5)	88 (2.6)	55 (4.1)	60 (4.5)	25 (4.6)

Calculator Task

Overall Task Average▼	Item 1 Perform Calculations	Item 2 Identify Pattern	Item 3 Predict: Routine Application	Item 4 Predict: Non-Routine Application	Item 5 Explain Predictions
48 (2.6)	96 (1.1)	27 (3.4)	56 (5.2)	37 (4.4)	21 (2.8)

Folding and Cutting Task

Overall Task Average▼	Item 1 Fold and Cut Shape 1	Item 2 Fold and Cut Shape 2	Item 3 Fold and Cut Shape 3
50 (3.3)	50 (3.8)	53 (3.3)	46 (4.2)

Around the Bend Task

Overall Task Average▼	Item 1 Measure Models	Item 2 Convert Using Scale	Item 3 Draw Models to Scale	Item 4 Solve Problem With Models
47 (3.3)	49 (5.1)	29 (4.8)	47 (5.0)	62 (3.9)

Packaging Task

Overall Task Average▼	Item 1 Draw Boxes	Item 2 Draw Nets	Item 3 Construct Net to Scale
28 (3.4)	25 (3.9)	28 (3.3)	33 (4.8)

SOURCE: IEA Third International Mathematics and Science Study (TIMSS), 1994-95.

* Percent of total possible points on each item averaged over students.

▼Average of percentage scores across items; all items weighted equally.

() Standard errors appear in parentheses. Because results are rounded to the nearest whole number, some totals may appear inconsistent.

Appendix

C

ACKNOWLEDGMENTS

TIMSS was truly a collaborative effort among hundreds of individuals around the world. Staff from the national research centers, the international management, advisors, and funding agencies worked closely to design and implement the most ambitious study of international comparative achievement ever undertaken. TIMSS would not have been possible without the tireless efforts of all involved. The TIMSS performance assessment was an integral part of the study and one that required a great deal of additional resources and effort for all involved in that component. The TIMSS Performance Assessment Committee is to be specially acknowledged for their contribution to this important undertaking, as are the countries that opted to administer the performance assessment. Below, the individuals and organizations are acknowledged for their contributions to TIMSS. Given that implementing TIMSS has spanned more than seven years and involved so many people and organizations, this list may not pay heed to all who contributed throughout the life of the project. Any omission is inadvertent. TIMSS also acknowledges the students, teachers, and school principals who contributed their time and effort to the study. This report would not be possible without them. Appreciation also is extended to Maria Sachs for her work editing this report.

MANAGEMENT AND OPERATIONS

Since 1993, TIMSS has been directed by the International Study Center at Boston College in the United States. Prior to this, the study was coordinated by the International Coordinating Center at the University of British Columbia in Canada. Although the study was directed centrally by the International Study Center and its staff members implemented various parts of TIMSS, important activities also were carried out in centers around the world. The data were processed centrally by the IEA Data Processing Center in Hamburg, Germany. Statistics Canada was responsible for collecting and evaluating the sampling documentation from each country and for calculating the sampling weights. The Australian Council for Educational Research conducted the scaling of the achievement data.

INTERNATIONAL STUDY CENTER (1993-)

Albert E. Beaton, International Study Director
Michael O. Martin, Deputy International Study Director
Ina V.S. Mullis, Co-Deputy International Study Director
Eugenio J. Gonzalez, Director of Operations and Data Analysis
Dana L. Kelly, Research Associate
Teresa A. Smith, Research Associate
Cheryl L. Flaherty, Research Associate
Maryellen Harmon, Performance Assessment Coordinator
Robert Jin, Computer Programmer
Ce Shen, Computer Programmer
William J. Crowley, Fiscal Administrator
Thomas M. Hoffmann, Publications Coordinator
Jonathan R. English, Systems Manager
José Rafael Nieto, Senior Production Specialist
Ann G.A. Tan, Conference Coordinator
Mary C. Howard, Office Supervisor
Diane Joyce, Secretary
Joanne E. McCourt, Secretary
Kathleen A. Haley, Graduate Assistant
Craig D. Hoyle, Graduate Assistant

INTERNATIONAL COORDINATING CENTER (1991-93)

David F. Robitaille, International Coordinator
Robert A. Garden, Deputy International Coordinator
Barry Anderson, Director of Operations
Beverley Maxwell, Director of Data Management

STATISTICS CANADA

Pierre Foy, Senior Methodologist
Suzelle Giroux, Senior Methodologist
Jean Dumais, Senior Methodologist
Nancy Darcovich, Senior Methodologist
Marc Joncas, Senior Methodologist
Laurie Reedman, Junior Methodologist
Claudio Perez, Junior Methodologist

IEA DATA PROCESSING CENTER

Jens Brockmann, Senior Researcher
Michael Bruneforth, Senior Researcher (former)
Jedidiah Harris, Research Assistant
Dirk Hastedt, Senior Researcher
Heiko Jungclaus, Senior Researcher
Svenja Moeller, Research Assistant
Knut Schwippert, Senior Researcher
Jockel Wolff, Research Assistant

AUSTRALIAN COUNCIL FOR EDUCATIONAL RESEARCH

Raymond J. Adams, Principal Research Fellow
Margaret Wu, Research Fellow
Nikolai Volodin, Research Fellow
David Roberts, Research Officer
Greg Macaskill, Research Officer

FUNDING AGENCIES

Funding for the International Study Center was provided by the National Center for Education Statistics of the U.S. Department of Education, the U.S. National Science Foundation, and the International Association for the Evaluation for Educational Achievement. Eugene Owen and Lois Peak of the National Center for Education Statistics and Larry Suter of the National Science Foundation each played a crucial role in making TIMSS possible and for ensuring the quality of the study. Funding for the International Coordinating Center was provided by the Applied Research Branch of the Strategic Policy Group of the Canadian Ministry of Human Resources Development. This initial source of funding was vital to initiate the TIMSS project. Tjeerd Plomp, Chair of the IEA and of the TIMSS International Steering Committee, has been a constant source of support throughout TIMSS. It should be noted that each country provided its own funding for the implementation of the study at the national level.

NATIONAL RESEARCH COORDINATORS

The TIMSS National Research Coordinators and their staff had the enormous task of implementing the TIMSS design in their countries. This required obtaining funding for the project; participating in the development of the instruments and procedures; conducting field tests; participating in and conducting training sessions; translating the instruments and procedural manuals into the local language; selecting the sample of schools and students; working with the schools to arrange for the testing; arranging for data collection, coding, and data entry; preparing the data files for submission to the IEA Data Processing Center; contributing to the development of the international reports; and preparing national reports. The way in which the national centers operated and the resources that were available varied considerably across the TIMSS countries. In some countries, the tasks were conducted centrally, while in others, various components were subcontracted to other organizations. In some countries, resources were more than adequate, while in others, the national centers were operating with limited resources. Of course, across the life of the project, some NRCs have changed. This list attempts to include all past NRCs who served for a significant period of time as well as all the present NRCs. All of the TIMSS National Research Coordinators and their staff members are to be commended for their professionalism and their dedication in conducting all aspects of TIMSS.

Argentina
Carlos Mansilla
Universidad del Chaco
Av. Italia 350
3500 Resistencia
Chaco, Argentina

Australia
Jan Lokan
Raymond Adams*
Australian Council for Educational Research
19 Prospect Hill
Private Bag 55
Camberwell, Victoria 3124
Australia

Austria
Guenter Haider
Austrian IEA Research Centre
Universität Salzburg
Akademiestraße 26/2
A-5020 Salzburg, Austria

Belgium (Flemish)
Christiane Brusselmans-Dehairs
Rijksuniversiteit Ghent
Vakgroep Onderwijskunde &
The Ministry of Education
Henri Dunantlaan 2
B-9000 Ghent, Belgium

Belgium (French)
Georges Henry
Christian Monseur
Université de Liège
B32 Sart-Tilman
4000 Liège 1, Belgium

Bulgaria
Kiril Bankov
Foundation for Research, Communication,
Education and Informatics
Tzarigradsko Shausse 125, Bl. 5
1113 Sofia, Bulgaria

Canada
Alan Taylor
Applied Research & Evaluation Services
University of British Columbia
2125 Main Mall
Vancouver, B.C. V6T 1Z4
Canada

Colombia
Carlos Jairo Diaz
Universidad del Valle
Facultad de Ciencias
Multitaller de Materiales Didacticos Ciudad
Universitaria Meléndez
Apartado Aereo 25360
Cali, Colombia

Cyprus
Constantinos Papanastasiou
Department of Education
University of Cyprus
Kallipoleos 75
P.O. Box 537
Nicosia CY-1789, Cyprus

Czech Republic
Jana Strakova
Vladislav Tomasek
Institute for Information on Education
Senovazne Nam. 26
111 21 Praha 1, Czech Republic

Denmark
Peter Weng
Peter Allerup
Borge Prien*
The Danish National Institute for
Educational Research
28 Hermodsgade
Dk-2200 Copenhagen N, Denmark

England
Wendy Keys
Derek Foxman*
National Foundation for
Educational Research
The Mere, Upton Park
Slough, Berkshire SL1 2DQ
England

France
Anne Servant
Ministère de l'Education Nationale
142, rue du Bac
75007 Paris, France

Josette Le Coq*
Centre International d'Etudes Pédagogiques
(CIEP)
1 Avenue Léon Journault
93211 Sèvres, France

*Past National Research Coordinator.

Germany
Rainer Lehmann
Humboldt-Universitaet zu Berlin
Institut fuer Allgemeine
Erziehungswissenschaft
Geschwister-Scholl-Str. 6
10099 Berlin, Germany

Juergen Baumert
Max-Planck Institute for Human
Development and Education
Lentzeallee 94
D-14195 Berlin, Germany

Manfred Lehrke
Universität Kiel
IPN
Olshausen Str. 62
24098 Kiel, Germany

Greece
Georgia Kontogiannopoulou-Polydorides
Department of Education
Tmima Nipiagogon
University of Athens
Navarinou 13, Neochimio
Athens 106 80, Greece

Joseph Solomon
Department of Education
University of Patras
Patras 26500, Greece

Hong Kong
Frederick Leung
Nancy Law
The University of Hong Kong
Department of Curriculum Studies
Pokfulam Road, Hong Kong

Hungary
Péter Vari
National Institute of Public Education
Centre for Evaluation Studies
Dorottya u. 8, P.F. 701/420
1051 Budapest, Hungary

Iceland
Einar Gudmundsson
Institute for Educational Research
Department of Educational Testing
and Measurement
Surdgata 39
101 Reykjavik, Iceland

Indonesia
Jahja Umar
Ministry of Education and Culture
Examination Development Center
Jalan Gunung Sahari - 4
Jakarta 10000, Indonesia

Ireland
Deirdre Stuart
Michael Martin*
Educational Research Centre
St. Patrick's College
Drumcondra
Dublin 9, Ireland

Iran, Islamic Republic
Ali Reza Kiamanesh
Ministry of Education
Center for Educational Research
Iranshahr Shomali Avenue
Teheran 15875, Iran

Israel
Pinchas Tamir
The Hebrew University
Israel Science Teaching Center
Jerusalem 91904, Israel

Ruth Zuzovsky
Tel Aviv University
School of Education
Ramat Aviv
PO Box 39040
Tel Aviv 69978, Israel

Italy
Anna Maria Caputo
Ministero della Pubblica Istruzione
Centro Europeo dell'Educazione
Villa Falconieri
00044 Frascati, Italy

Japan
Masao Miyake
Eizo Nagasaki
National Institute for Educational Research
6-5-22 Shimomeguro
Meguro-Ku, Tokyo 153, Japan

Korea
Jingyu Kim
Hyung Im*
National Board of Educational Evaluation
Research Division
15-1 Chungdam-2 dong, Kangnam-ku Seoul
135-102, Korea

Kuwait
Mansour Hussein
Ministry of Education
P.O. Box 7
Safat 13001, Kuwait

Latvia
Andrejs Geske
University of Latvia
Faculty of Education & Psychology
Jurmalas gatve 74/76, Rm. 204A
Riga, LV-1083, Latvia

Lithuania
Algirdas Zabulionis
National Examination Centre
Ministry of Education & Science
M. Katkaus 44
2006 Vilnius, Lithuania

Mexico
Fernando Córdova Calderón
Director de Evaluación de Politicas y
Sistemas Educativos
Netzahualcoyotl #127 2ndo Piso
Colonia Centro
Mexico 1, D.F., Mexico

Netherlands
Wilmad Kuiper
Anja Knuver
Klaas Bos
University of Twente
Faculty of Educational Science
and Technology
Department of Curriculum
P.O. Box 217
7500 AE Enschede, Netherlands

New Zealand
Hans Wagemaker
Megan Chamberlain
Steve May
Robyn Caygill
Ministry of Education
Research Section
Private Box 1666
45-47 Pipitea Street
Wellington, New Zealand

Norway
Svein Lie
University of Oslo
SLS
Postboks 1099 Blindern
0316 Oslo 3, Norway

Gard Brekke
Alf Andersensv 13
3670 Notodden, Norway

Philippines
Milagros Ibe
University of the Philippines
Institute for Science and Mathematics
Education Development
Diliman, Quezon City
Philippines

Ester Ogena
Science Education Institute
Department of Science and Technology
Bicutan, Taquig
Metro Manila 1604, Philippines

Portugal
Gertrudes Amaro
Ministerio da Educacao
Instituto de Inovação Educacional
Rua Artilharia Um 105
1070 Lisboa, Portugal

Romania
Gabriela Noveanu
Institute for Educational Sciences
Evaluation and Forecasting Division
Str. Stirbei Voda 37
70732-Bucharest, Romania

Russian Federation
Galina Kovalyova
The Russian Academy of Education
Institute of General Secondary School
Ul. Pogodinskaya 8
Moscow 119905, Russian Federation

Scotland
Brian Semple
Scottish Office
Education & Industry Department
Victoria Quay
Edinburgh, E86 6QQ
Scotland

Singapore
Chan Siew Eng
Research and Evaluation Branch
Block A Belvedere Building
Ministry of Education
Kay Siang Road
Singapore 248922

Slovak Republic
Maria Berova
Vladimir Burjan*
SPU-National Institute for Education
Pluhova 8
P.O. Box 26
830 00 Bratislava
Slovak Republic

Slovenia
Marjan Setinc
Center for IEA Studies
Educational Research Institute
Gerbiceva 62, P.O. Box 2976
61111 Ljubljana, Slovenia

South Africa
Derek Gray
Human Sciences Research Council
134 Pretorius Street
Private Bag X41
Pretoria 0001, South Africa

Spain
José Antonio Lopez Varona
Instituto Nacional de Calidad y Evaluación
C/San Fernando del Jarama No. 14
28002 Madrid, Spain

Sweden
Ingemar Wedman
Anna Hofslagare
Kjell Gisselberg*
Umeå University
Department of Educational Measurement S-
901 87 Umeå, Sweden

Switzerland
Erich Ramseier
Amt Für Bildungsforschung der
Erziehungsdirektion des Kantons Bern
Sulgeneck Straße 70
Ch-3005 Bern, Switzerland

Thailand
Suwaporn Semheng
Institute for the Promotion of Teaching
Science and Technology
924 Sukhumvit Road
Bangkok 10110, Thailand

United States
William Schmidt
Michigan State University
Department of Educational Psychology
463 Erikson Hall
East Lansing, MI 48824-1034
United States

TIMSS ADVISORY COMMITTEES

The International Study Center was supported in its work by several advisory committees. The International Steering Committee provided guidance to the International Study Director on policy issues and general direction of the study. The TIMSS Technical Advisory Committee provided guidance on issues related to design, sampling, instrument construction, analysis, and reporting, ensuring that the TIMSS methodologies and procedures were technically sound. The Subject Matter Advisory Committee ensured that current thinking in mathematics and science education were addressed by TIMSS, and was instrumental in the development of the TIMSS tests. The Free-Response Item Coding Committee developed the coding rubrics for the free-response items. The Performance Assessment Committee worked with the Performance Assessment Coordinator to develop the TIMSS performance assessment. The Quality Assurance Committee helped to develop the quality assurance program.

INTERNATIONAL STEERING COMMITTEE

Tjeerd Plomp (Chair), the Netherlands
Lars Ingelstam, Sweden
Daniel Levine, United States
Senta Raizen, United States
David Robitaille, Canada
Toshio Sawada, Japan
Benny Suprapto Brotosiswojo, Indonesia
William Schmidt, United States

TECHNICAL ADVISORY COMMITTEE

Raymond Adams, Australia
Pierre Foy, Canada
Andreas Schleicher, Germany
William Schmidt, United States
Trevor Williams, United States

SAMPLING REFEREE

Keith Rust, United States

SUBJECT AREA COORDINATORS

Robert Garden, New Zealand (Mathematics)
Graham Orpwood, Canada (Science)

SPECIAL MATHEMATICS CONSULTANT

Chancey Jones

SUBJECT MATTER ADVISORY COMMITTEE

Svein Lie (Chair), Norway
Antoine Bodin, France
Peter Fensham, Australia
Robert Garden, New Zealand
Geoffrey Howson, England
Curtis McKnight, United States
Graham Orpwood, Canada
Senta Raizen, United States
David Robitaille, Canada
Pinchas Tamir, Israel
Alan Taylor, Canada
Ken Travers, United States
Theo Wubbels, the Netherlands

FREE-RESPONSE ITEM CODING COMMITTEE

Svein Lie (Chair), Norway
Vladimir Burjan, Slovak Republic
Kjell Gisselberg, Sweden
Galina Kovalyova, Russian Federation
Nancy Law, Hong Kong
Josette Le Coq, France
Jan Lokan, Australia
Curtis McKnight, United States
Graham Orpwood, Canada
Senta Raizen, United States
Alan Taylor, Canada
Peter Weng, Denmark
Algirdas Zabulionis, Lithuania

PERFORMANCE ASSESSMENT COMMITTEE

Derek Foxman, England
Robert Garden, New Zealand
Per Morten Kind, Norway
Svein Lie, Norway
Jan Lokan, Australia
Graham Orpwood, Canada

QUALITY ASSURANCE COMMITTEE

Jules Goodison, United States
Hans Pelgrum, The Netherlands
Ken Ross, Australia

EDITORIAL COMMITTEE

David F. Robitaille (Chair), Canada
Albert Beaton, International Study Director
Paul Black, England
Svein Lie, Norway
Rev. Ben Nebres, Philippines
Judith Torney-Purta, United States
Ken Travers, United States
Theo Wubbels, the Netherlands

Art Direction and Cover Design by Thomas M. Hoffmann

Table Production by José R. Nieto